SPECTACULAR
TEAMWORK

SPECTACULAR TEAMWORK

How To Develop the Leadership Skills for Team Success

ROBERT R. BLAKE
JANE S. MOUTON
ROBERT L. ALLEN

John Wiley & Sons

NEW YORK · CHICHESTER · BRISBANE · TORONTO · SINGAPORE

This publication is designed to provide accurate and authoritative information in
regard to the subject matter covered. It is sold with the understanding that the
publisher is not engaged in rendering legal, accounting, or other professional
service. If legal advice or other expert assistance is required, the services of a
competent professional person should be sought. *From a Declaration of Principles
jointly adopted by a Committee of the American Bar Association and a Committee
of Publishers.*

Library of Congress Cataloging in Publication Data:

Blake, Robert Rogers, 1918-
  Spectacular teamwork.

  Bibliography: p.
  Includes index.
  1. Work groups.   I. Mouton, Jane Srygley.   II. Title
HD66.B54 1987   658.4'036   86-28123
ISBN 0-471-85311-9

Printed in the United States of America
10 9 8 7 6 5 4 3 2 1

Preface

Human effectiveness is something that everyone wants. It is universally appreciated when it is achieved. There are two ways to increase human effectiveness: (1) concentrate on the individual and (2) focus on the team. In modern organizations, the vast majority of people work in teams and almost no one works in total isolation from others. For most people, achieving successful results depends on how well they and others with whom they work are able to mesh effort. Thus because of the increased importance teamwork has taken on, it is the focus of this book.

Individuals with strong, positive personalities may be described by their co-workers as "excellent" or "very effective." This is one reason why selection and development of individuals receives so much emphasis. But when effective individuals interact, they may or may not produce an effective team. One-upmanship, working at cross-purposes, paying lip service to the boss, sloppy standards for what constitutes effective performance, unclear goals and objectives, and so on, may interfere. Team performance can only be productive if the team culture is strong and positive.

The starting point for developing teamwork is for each member of the team to understand both the dynamics of teamwork and the basic dimensions by which a team's performance can be measured. When the concept of truly excellent teamwork is understood by members, the understanding can be used to improve their own performance—sometimes with dramatic speed. The concepts and methods presented here strengthen the possibility of participation by providing organization members an understanding of what it is, what it isn't, what is required in insight and understanding, and what is required in behavioral skills for effectiveness.

Six of the illustrations provided in the following chapters are real-life situations in which actual work teams experience problems that impede the development of participation. A seventh illustration provides a concrete example of what teamwork feels like when it is at its very best. It serves as a model for thinking about the real issues of effective teamwork.

After each team culture illustration, there is a series of diagnostic scales to evaluate how closely your team matches the example. This is a working manual that permits you to match the teamwork that goes on in your team with these various illustrations of both sound and unsound teamwork. Then you can distinguish between what your team is and is not doing well—and what to do to close any gaps. Sometimes this kind of gap closing takes the active participation of every team member—that's what team building is all about.

The latter part of this book describes various team-building approaches for bringing about effectiveness. It offers an explanation of what each member or team may do to strengthen participation and contribute to the effective participation of others.

ROBERT R. BLAKE
JANE S. MOUTON
ROBERT L. ALLEN

Austin, Texas
January, 1987

Contents

Contents

SPECTACULAR TEAMWORK

Chapter One

Effective Participation Is the Key to Sound Teamwork

No question about it, a change is in the air. The change: mobilizing human resources for strengthened results, productivity, quality, creativity, and innovation. The goals: better profit, sustained growth, and effective competition in a global economy. The changes involved go to the heart of teamwork itself. It can no longer be assumed that effective teamwork will occur if sufficiently talented personnel are joined in a common task even when the objectives are clear. Sports history is rife with examples of the failure of teams to perform successfully despite the fact that every effort was made to assemble as many "superstars" as possible in order to win. The "chemistry" wasn't right; the stars were unable to integrate their efforts toward the overall goal of team victory. That same chemistry seems to be missing in organization teams as well. Individual talent is, of course, indispensable for the success of any organization. But, perhaps for the first time on a wide scale, organizations are coming to realize that their talent is, at best, underutilized and frequently wasted.

There is almost universal agreement about what kind of change is needed. Strengthened participation by all organization members — up and down and sideways on the organizational chart — is the factor that can make the difference.

Who says so?

Drucker,[1] Iacocca,[2] Crosby,[3,4] Peters,[5,6] Geneen,[7] Ouchi,[8] Naisbitt,[9] international unions, and the Japanese say so. Marshall McLuhan called it The Global Village.[10] And informed managers are beginning to say so. When a group of such diverse people is in agreement, you have to believe them! This unanimity of opinion is unique. In the past, diversity of opinion obscured organizational ills.

It is one thing, though, to know what is important for

bringing about improvement and a different thing to effect it. It can be taken for granted that most organization members want to participate as fully and productively as possible, and that something blocks this happening. So why has it proven so difficult to strengthen the quantity and quality of participation? Why have so many approaches somehow or other either failed or produced mixed results? Increased participation has not been achieved by emulation of "excellence," (as advocated by Peters[5,6]) or by vicarious association. Similarly, Blanchard's[11] recommendation that judiciously employed praise and reprimand during a series of one-minute contacts with subordinates can stimulate improved involvement and commitment has met with mixed reviews. Other attempts at getting participation that have suffered similar fates include quality circles, brainstorming, Theory Z, and so on. Approaches that have increased in popularity have had their day and waned.

The common feature behind all these approaches is that they use direct means to bring about improved participation. They use either persuasive appeals, direct manipulation through reward and reprimand, or "repeal" of conventional authority relations. None has aimed at strengthening participation by providing members skills of effective behavior essential for participating in a responsible manner; none offers organization members greater insight into the barriers that arise within their team cultures; none say what to do.

Some Reasons That Teamwork Is Essential

Many organizations have come to realize that people are their most important strategic resource. Although such credos have been paid lip service for years, the emerging forces of this postindustrial world — such as computers and deregulation — now require serious consideration.

Computer access to operating information has eliminated the need to funnel information through the narrow channels of a hierarchical organization. The computer is smashing the pyramid, reducing the number of layers, and replacing line managers with information access. Participation skills are necessary to exploit this breakthrough.

The global trading community now brings a sharp challenge to those who have utilized people and managers as tools of production. There are people in other countries who will work for lower wages. Worse yet, many foreign countries appear to have developed management philosophies that are superior to our own. Their skills for effective participation are better.

Deregulation has produced yet another factor. Regulation is written authoritarianism. New areas of freedom of action and entrepreneurship have emerged and skills of participation have become even more essential to success.

Much has been written about excellence and vision in organizations. Undoubtedly there is merit in presenting a model or an ideal. However, when an attempt is made to bring the ideal into use, it collides with the existing culture. The following discussion outlines this issue.

Excellence in Teamwork

Over the years we have studied many organizations — their cultures, leaders, members, and work groups. Every so often we were able to observe a team that transcended its organizational limitations to realize results that far exceeded the norms of the organization. It was intriguing to speculate about what caused such superlative performance and what could be done by other groups to replicate it.

The Role of Leadership

Generally the problem lies in the leadership itself or in the extant team culture.

Leaders usually provide a vision of future possibilities. That is an essential aspect of leadership. But an equally important dimension of leadership is ensuring teamwork. Most current strategies for doing so include use of power to edict compliance, use of reward to moderate resistance, and use of negotiation to attain a position short of the ideal. It is far more effective to elicit employee participation in the creation of the vision than to impose the vision on the team. Such input gives team membership a proprietary feeling. This seems like a simple solution, but it demands the leader and other team members have skills that may not be present — skills of participation.

If the leader has not provided vision, the team then will drift from day to day in a survival mode. The vision may exist in whole or in part in several minds, but the cultural norms of the team resist its emergence. Again, participation skills can create legitimacy to the notion of vision and possibilities.

The Role of Teamwork

No matter where the problems lie an effort should be made to alleviate them. Team building means taking deliberate action to identify and remove barriers and to replace unsound behavior with the kind that can lead to superlative performance. Absence of vision exacerbates the feelings of dissatisfaction with the current state of affairs and helplessness to effect the needed changes. A feeling of "them-ism" emerges: others get the blame and become a source of unrest and an excuse for inaction.

Teamwork is a plural process. It cannot be done by one person. When people come together to form groups, each member brings a personal set of knowledge, skills, values, and motivations. How these interact to form a collectivity can be positive or negative. In some cases members neutralize each other to produce ineffectiveness or inaction. The whole becomes less than the sum of its parts. In other cases they can be partly or wholly additive. There is yet another possibility: the interaction can stimulate a transcendent state that exceeds the contribution of any member or the sum of all the members. When that happens, the team has achieved synergy. The whole is greater than the sum of its parts. The team result has exceeded the sum of individual contribution; that's the meaning of excellence in teamwork when teamwork becomes spectacular.

Let's use the following "spectacular teamwork" as an example. A manager and a subordinate are making a decision. They both studied a technical document whose contents provide the facts, data, and logic underlying a needed complex decision.

Suppose it were possible to give each person an objective test about what he or she knows of the technical document before they begin to discuss the decision. On a 100-item test one of them receives a score of 50 and the other a score of 70.

When they begin discussion, they might cancel one another out and, in such a way, cause confusion and uncertainty as to the facts, data, and logic needed for a sound decision. This might reduce the average score of 60 to possibly 45 on completion of the discussion. This would mean that they had reached a new level of misunderstanding as a result of the discussion which was below the best understanding of either of the individuals prior to their discussion. That's not spectacular.

On the other hand, they might pool their thinking and take the average of their two understandings as the basis for the decision. In this case the action taken would be represented by a score of 60 — above the poorest that would have been done by the less prepared individual but below the understanding of the better prepared of the two individuals. That's not spectacular either.

A third possibility exists. As manager and subordinate begin discussing the correct answers to the questions on the basis of *mutual understanding,* it turns out that the manager has certain correct understandings that the subordinate lacks. Equally, the subordinate has certain critical insights that are unavailable to the manager. Each shares understanding and they go on to discuss gray areas where neither is clear as to the best answer. During the open and candid discussion each is able to help the other to think through to a clear-cut understanding of what is involved in terms of facts, data, and logic for reaching a sound decision. Thus a final score on the test after discussion is 99.

If the average of their two individual scores on the test were taken without discussion, the average amount of facts, data, and logic available to them would have been 60. If the decision had been made by the better prepared one, it would have been based on a 70 score of understanding. From this open and candid discussion, they were able to raise the level of understanding to 99; far above either's comprehension of the facts, data, and logic prior to the discussion.

This kind of performance is spectacular for many reasons. First, we see two people working together in the interest of achieving a common goal—getting the best solution. What's more they do it.

They do it by listening to one another, by correlating information and confirming it when both agree, and by identifying those areas in which they are not in agreement and examining why each thinks in a different way. They are also willing to admit when they are uncertain about a position. The aim is to identify and clarify any faulty data or assumptions. They do it by challenging one another, confronting one another, or contradicting one another but all in an open and candid way and toward the singular purpose of finding the soundest solution. This permits one or the other to abandon a prior conviction that was mistaken without feeling "defeated."

This is spectacular, particularly when you realize that one of them is the manager of the other. The manager is in a position to pull rank, impose personal judgments, force compliance, smooth over differences, or go along with halfway solutions. But it doesn't happen. Why? Because the manager wants, values, and respects the subordinate's input.

This kind of spectacular teamwork means both are involved and committed. The quality of participation between them is based on a solid foundation of give and take, and a readiness to resist jumping at the first answer, the easy answer, or the convenient answer in order to get the best answer.

That's between two people. When you realize that much teamwork involves five, six, or more people, you can appreciate what a significant achievement it is when several can work in the synergistic way that's characteristic of these two.

All that, however, is an evaluation of their performance from an organizational point of view. What's the evaluation from a personal angle? When people are able to grapple with a difficult and complex problem and come out of it with something far better than could have been had without the joint effort, the emotional reaction is one of deep satisfaction. There is something at the very core of human experience that finds gratification from that kind of performance. Those involved have not only proved it can be done but also that they can do it. It reinforces a person's feelings of self-value and creates a willingness among people to be mutually supportive of one another in future efforts.

Synergistic teamwork is smart teamwork. It offers corporations perhaps the greatest single possibility for strengthening effectiveness through mobilizing human resources. Getting the maximum benefits from commitment, involvement, strong initiative, good inquiry, open advocacy, effective conflict resolution, solid decision making, and extensive use of critique is what spectacular teamwork is all about.

Synergy and Teamwork

The notion of synergy is intriguing from a team perspective. It requires both individual contribution and awareness and respect for that of others. It cannot be ordered forth by authority or be a product of indifference. Compromise destroys the possibility of its emergence. Warmth and mutual support are palliatives that deny its happening. Only when concern for a team result is integrated with trust and mutual support among members is synergy likely to emerge.

Synergy is the vision that is within reach of every team in every organization. It can become the attainable standard for team achievement. Given that we know a lot of what not to do, what course can be productive? What can leaders and team members do to elicit and sustain productivity, creativity, and innovation? How can they each be a source and a product of synergy?

The answer lies in the team. Each member, including the leader, needs to assume responsibility for creating a vision — that is, to adopt it as his or her own and share responsibility for achieving it.

Strategies of Teamwork

Before continuing it is necessary to clarify an important point — from a strategic point of view, when teamwork is desired, there are five different tactical approaches to teamwork: (1) one alone, (2) one to one, (3) one to some, (4) one to all, and (5) all to one.

When managers think about the dynamics of teamwork, they often assume (incorrectly) that teamwork occurs only under face-to-face conditions, when all team members are present in one place. They think of meetings, task forces, or similar one-to-all situations. They may assume as a corollary that any one-alone or solo action is not teamwork. Such assumptions are invalid, for both one-alone and one-to-all actions are an important part of good teamwork. For example, in some teams one-alone action may be dominant, with each person working alone, whereas one-to-all approaches are used infrequently and only then to "touch base." Or a task may require one-to-one interaction in which two team members work together at a given time. Sometimes one-to-some interactions are needed, with several but not all team members working together on a problem. The one-to-all approach is employed when a task requires the involvement of all team members. There is one additional aspect of teamwork. The all-to-one approach occurs when team members focus attention on one person to help this individual strengthen personal effectiveness as a unit of the team.

Smoothly functioning teams use all five approaches to teamwork. The choice of a particular approach is tactical. It depends on the situation and the problem to be solved. Persons outside the team are brought into problem solving when they can contribute significantly to final decisions or when their understanding and commitment are vital to ensure effective implementation. No approach is in itself more effective than another. In any case, the manager maintains leadership, authority, and responsibility for decisions.

Team Leadership

There is no question that the team leader bears the ultimate responsibility for success. The issue lies in whether the exercise of leadership uses the resources of the team effectively to produce positive results. Leaders interpret the mandate of their responsibility in different ways:

- Some believe in exercise of authority to extract compliance.
- Some consider that a contented, conflict-free team can be most productive.
- Some interpret their role in a hierarchical sense to handle the flow of messages and orders from above.

In most cases leaders have had to come to grips with risks inherent in exercising authority. They may have accommodated their authority by moderating it, rationalizing, trading off favorable benefits, or hiding their true motives.

As team members respond to the leadership in various ways, their own values come into play. Sooner or later, as norms are formed and each team member develops standards of performance and expectations of himself or herself and the others, a team culture emerges. The process may be an easy accommodative one or one tortured with conflict, turnover, and replacement. It is also possible to transcend issues of authority in pursuit of higher goals. The leader and members may become so attracted to the ideal of a desirable future state that commitment to pursue it is unbridled. The process of changing from "what we are now" to "what we could be" is not simple. However, like all tasks, there are ways of going about it that have greater assurance of success. The final measures of success are straightforward:

- Collectively achieved productivity
- Creativity and innovation elicited through both doing things right and doing right things
- Satisfaction for team members

Whether a leader is a first level supervisor or chief executive officer, the process is the same. And the leader's responsibility to both the organization and the members of the team will be fulfilled.

How to Recognize Team Culture

Culture can be recognized by examining the attitudes, beliefs, and opinions that people communicate to one another on a day-in and day-out basis. Culture includes the traditions, precedents, and long-established practices that have become customs for interrelating and solving problems. These are the rules and guidelines that tell members how to participate, what to do, and what not to do. The following is an example of how team culture affects a work team.

Cindy Washington and Sam Blanks are department managers in a large manufacturing plant. It is autonomous in the sense that it is responsible for manufacturing as well as marketing, sales, distribution, and financial control of its products. Cindy and Sam have just come from a meeting of the plant manager and key department heads in which Cindy submitted a proposal for a new product launch.

The late afternoon sun cast long, stark shadows across the quadrangle. A shower of leaves, like golden coins, fell across the walk the two executives were following. They walked in step and in silence, their eyes down, each carrying a thick file. Suddenly, Cindy turned and spoke.

CINDY: Sam, I'm thinking of leaving the company.

SAM: You're kidding, Cindy.

CINDY: No, I've had it. I don't know where I'm going to go, but I've had it up to here with this running dogfight.

SAM: Dogfight?

CINDY: Sure, you saw what it was like today.

SAM: Just like any other day as far as I can see.

CINDY: Yeah, and that's just what I mean. But today was a special case for me. I worked night and day on that proposal, and you saw how it went. It's the whole atmosphere. And there doesn't seem to be any hope. I like a good argument, but what we're doing is not productive. It takes a lot longer to push something through than it does to develop it. And even when it's done, the end result is a watered-down version of a good solution. Look at today and tell me — honestly — if it was any different than last week, or the week before, or the week before that.

SAM: Well, you've got a point there.

CINDY: Yeah. In the end, we just blew two hours in frustration — a bunch of kids trying to get their own way. I've got better things to do. Look at my notepad. I measure the quality of the day by the absence of doodles — there isn't a place left to scrawl. In the end, Will, our fair-haired friend from finance, took the big lead. The others were too tired of fighting. And what resulted? No real answer. There wasn't a grain of substance left in the end decision. It stank. And all because no one wanted to give in.

Cindy is discussing team culture. One thing is certain, Cindy is not happy with her membership. As a matter of fact, she's so unhappy, she's going to leave. The cause of her unhappiness is the character of participation within the team. But when Cindy's situation is viewed in another way, what's really going on?

Two very fundamental issues are involved in Cindy's dilemma. One is power and authority, how conflict is dealt with in her team, and what it does to everyone's participation. The other is the uniformity of response, that is, the prevailing norms that determine how the members of the group interact with one another. These two fundamental issues of organizational psychology are at the very heart of the matter of participation.

We recognize that almost universal agreement exists that increased participation is the key for solving problems of productivity, quality, creativity, satisfaction, and so on. So why not simply put it on the line and let everybody know that they should work for increased participation, that it is expected of them, and that they will be rewarded in accordance with how much of it they get?

That seems to be where difficulties begin. It is one thing to want participation and another thing to create the conditions under which widespread participation becomes characteristic. Something more is required than an edict, pronouncement, or reward. This leads to the question, "What barriers have to be removed to achieve the degree of participation wanted?"

There seem to be two preconditions for participation: (1) How authority is exercised in the team. Remember, some ways of exercising authority stifle or kill participation and others release it. (2) Pressures to conform in the group. Informal norms, by which people in groups regulate their interactions, may be adverse to participation or to change from one level of participation to another. Members are more likely to conform to what is expected of them than to suffer the risk of being seen as troublemakers, nonadapters, or intractables exercising so much independence as to be out of control. Any approach to elicit stronger and more effective participation is confronted with dealing with these two factors that may prevent the wanted participation from appearing.

References

1. Drucker, Peter F. *Managing in Turbulent Times.* New York: Harper & Row, 1980.
2. Iacocca, Lee A., with Novak, William. *Iacocca: An Autobiography.* New York: Bantam, 1984.
3. Crosby, Philip B. *Quality Is Free: The Art of Making Quality Certain.* New York: McGraw-Hill, 1979.

4. Crosby, Philip B. *Quality Without Tears: The Art of Hassle-Free Management*. New York: McGraw-Hill, 1984.

5. Peters, Thomas J., and Waterman, Robert H. *In Search of Excellence: Lessons from America's Best-Run Companies*. New York: Harper & Row, 1982.

6. Peters, Thomas J., and Austin, Nancy K. *A Passion for Excellence: The Leadership Difference*. New York: Random House, 1985.

7. Geneen, Harold, and Moscow, Alvin. *Managing*. Garden City, NJ: Doubleday, 1984.

8. Ouchi, William G. *Theory Z: How American Business Can Meet the Japanese Challenge*. Reading, MA: Addison-Wesley, 1981.

9. Naisbitt, John, and Aburdene, Patricia. *Re-inventing the Corporation: Transforming Your Job and Your company for the New Information Society*. New York: Warner, 1985.

10. McLuhan, Marshall. *Understanding Media: The Extensions of Man*. New York: McGraw-Hill, 1964.

11. Blanchard, Kenneth H., and Johnson, Spencer. *The One-Minute Manager*. New York: Morrow, 1982.

Chapter Two

Battle Fatigue

The Importance of Common Objectives

L et's go back to the conversation between Cindy and Sam. Cindy had just said that the meeting was awful because no one wanted to give in. As they entered the heavy glass doors of the Technical Center, Sam responded to Cindy's statement.

SAM: Well, this is serious, Cindy. I think we should talk this through a bit. I know we had a pretty heavy session, but isn't that the price of excellence? You know Alan pushes every subject.

CINDY: That's just the point. The push has nothing to do with excellence. The whole team is full of counterpunchers.

They reached the heavy plain oak door of Sam's office and pushed it open. Inside, on the small round conference table, a fresh pot of coffee steamed. Sam tossed his file on the desk. They sat opposite each other and Sam poured.

SAM: You're probably the brightest systems person in the company. We've got to get to the bottom of this. You can't just sulk and quit. We need you — especially now. What's really troubling you? Why do you call our team "counterpunchers"?

CINDY: Take John, for example. He's so afraid of failure that he nitpicks a proposal to death. He misses the thrust and digs at little trivialities that don't matter a pinch. It's not perfectionism, it's raw fear. He's terrified at the thought of agreement and action.

SAM: I see what you're driving at.

CINDY: And Bob. He is numero uno in his own mind. He's got to run everything. He is so concerned with keeping everything his way that he just can't let another team member take the lead.

SAM: Score two for the sage; I never thought about it like that.

CINDY: You saw what happened today. It was cut and thrust and counterpunch all the way. Not only with me. He twisted your product idea until it fit his own. And remember the set-to between Bob and George. Red faces. Table thumping. A real standoff.

SAM: Gee, Alan tried.

CINDY: And then it became a three-way dogfight. We spent over two hours on that subject. The rest of us tried to break it up, but the resolution was impossible. A straw of an idea — a little bit of George, a little of Bob, a little of the boss — to break the impasse. Honestly now, do you think that will fly? No one has any commitment to it. It was just relief from three guys together slashing away at each other. Mark my words. That plan will either float up at the next meeting or die in the implementation.

SAM: Well, Alan tries to manage the differences by calling a halt to arguments, and I admire his readiness to let the team be a battlefield rather than to declare his solution the winner.

CINDY: When things reach an impasse, Alan does try to call the shots. But he lets people answer back, and you have to admire that.

SAM: Well, at least it's better than last year when he dealt with everyone individually.

CINDY: Yeah. It almost brought us to a halt. Each of us did our own thing and none of the interfaces fit.

SAM: I remember. We sure got hung up . . . . Do you think we should avoid conflict?

CINDY: Sam, you know as well as I do that I don't avoid conflict. But it has got to be constructive to make any progress. Closed minds, poor listening, repeating past arguments, and standoffs don't lead to productive conflict.

SAM: Have you talked to Alan about it?

CINDY: I've tried. But he smothers me with advice and never really hears. His mind is so busy with the need to control his team he can't see the picture. I came out feeling guilty about my criticism. I feel guilty right now. Heck, Sam, I like the guys — but we're killing each other.

Sam stared at his hands. Then he followed with:

SAM: You know, I can't really fault anything you say. I used to have the same concerns. I tried to break it up a couple of times. Now, I guess, I'm just used to it. It's our culture and I guess we're stuck with it. We're a bunch of strong characters. Oh, the boss comes out for innovative solutions once in a while, but we see the light for about one session and snap right back into our old ways. I used to think how great it would be if we wised up. There is a lot of waste of time and ideas. Most of our decisions are trade-offs. There's no commitment.

It's beginning to show, too. Sales are down six points and the opposition has made an end-run around us on the last two military bids. Alan is under the gun; headquarters isn't happy. The only time we unite is when we make a common enemy. Maybe we should ask the human resources department for help.

CINDY: No way! The problem is ours. If we can't solve it, nobody can.

SAM: But, I can't stand here and listen to you talk about leaving.

CINDY: Well, I feel better now, but I still think I should look around. This ship is going to sink and I don't want that on my resume.

SAM: What do you say we both talk to Alan in the morning?

CINDY: I don't know. It's got to get in front of the whole team. But I guess it's the only legitimate start. He really is a good guy. But I don't think he'd be warm to a revolt.

SAM: Tell you what. You think about it overnight. I'll meet you for coffee at Clancy's at 7:00.

CINDY: Okay, Sam, but I have to tell you, I don't see the way out. Will you look at the time! I've got to run. Thanks for listening.

This team is full of counterpunching rather than problem solving. Constructive critique and feedback are drowned out by blaming and shouting matches. The constant fighting leads to poor decisions and compromises rather than constructive confrontation and discussion of the issues. Alan, as the boss, does not take responsibility for teamwide problem solving. Instead he singles out individuals to talk to alone as a way of staying in control. As a result the team's morale is very low. Just about the only time their spirits pick up is when they find a common enemy.

The team members cannot agree on a set of common goals and objectives, making it virtually impossible to divide the workload in a strategically sensible way. The boss often issues job assignments by decree, without the benefit of any consultation about the best way to handle the workload. Excellence is scarce in such a group.

The Teamwork Grid®

Sound teamwork produces success in the important result areas of productivity, creativity, and satisfaction. Unsound teamwork produces shortfalls. Two important aspects of success emerge—content and process. Content is the subject matter to which the team applies its efforts. It is the aggregate of knowledge, skills, information, and insight the team utilizes in achieving its results. Process is the way teams go about using content—the dynamics that develop in setting standards of performance, in sharing responsibilities, in setting goals, in dividing up efforts, in interacting, and in reviewing the consequences of the team's actions. Although it is possible to improve content, process has the greatest potential for improvement.

The Teamwork Grid®, as shown in Figure 2.1, is a systematic way of analyzing the underlying patterns. By using the Teamwork Grid®, a team can develop a perception of where it is now and where it wants to be.

The Teamwork Grid® is a two-dimensional framework. Concern for production, that is, getting results, is one dimension. The second dimension is concern for people—superiors, colleagues, and subordinates—with and through whom the team achieves results. Concern is not a mechanical measure of production or conduct toward people. Rather it indicates the character or strength of the collective assumptions and values behind any group approach.

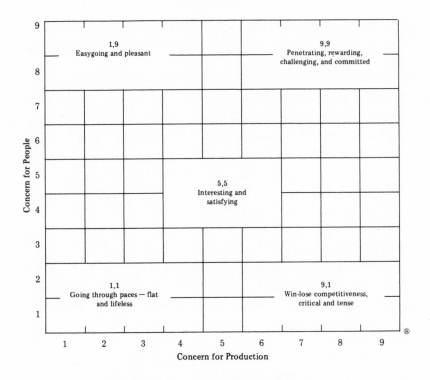

Figure 2.1. The Teamwork Grid®

A team may demonstrate concern for production (or results) by defining quantitative objectives, by insistence for their achievement, by exploring new means for efficiency, or by adopting new methods of handling content. Production is whatever an organization employs people to accomplish.

Since results are accomplished with and through others, assumptions made about people are important in determining effectiveness. Concern for people is demonstrated in many ways, including mutual trust and support, participation, ensuring understanding, open communication, respect and attitude toward working conditions, benefits, and equity in salary administration.

Depending on the character of concern, team members may respond with enthusiasm or resentment, involvement or apathy, innovation or dull response, commitment or resistance, eagerness or hesitation. The Teamwork Grid® measures these concerns on a 9-point scale. Low concern is a 1, an average amount of concern is a 5, and high concern is a 9. The manner in which team values come together defines the quality of team action. Clarifying the available options helps a team to understand where it is now and what choices it has available.

Although there are many possible ways in which these two concerns come together, seven combinations are especially important in understanding the culture of a team. These are the benchmark styles:

1. *9,1 — Maximum concern for production; minimum concern for people.* Individual and collective concern for results predominate over concern for people. The resulting operational culture is likely to be one of conflict, one-upmanship, antagonism, competition, and criticism.

2. *1,9 — Minimum concern for production; maximum concern for people.* Fostering good feelings takes precedence over operational results. Teams become concerned with rewards and benefits, working conditions, comfort, friendliness, and the avoidance of conflict.

3. *1,1 — Minimum concern exists for both production and people.* Survival becomes the mode of the team and responses are calculated to ensure compliance with orders

and objectives from above. Self-protection, individuality, low tolerance for risk are likely to be cultural norms.

4. *5,5 — Average amounts of concern on both scales produces a middle-of-the-road attitude.* "Teamness" is frequently the product as status quo is saluted and team members resort to rules and policies to minimize conflict and ensure acceptability and conformity to the organization and to each other.

5. *9,9 — Both concerns are integrated at a high level in a team approach.* The team and its members are goal-oriented and seek results by participation, involvement, and commitment of all those who can contribute.

6. *9+9 — Paternalism — Concerns are high for both results and people, but in an additive way.* This means that rather than an integration of the two concerns at a high level as in 9,9, a high concern for production is followed by a high concern for people when desired results are achieved. Thus the two concerns, although simultaneously present, are applied separately.

   The dominant 9,1 authoritarian pursuit of control is offset by treating people well in terms of salaries, benefits, working relations. This style is leader- or organization-oriented with a strong undercurrent of control. There are rewards for compliance and criticism or rejection for noncompliance. The reward relieves the leader of guilt that may be associated with failure to involve, and the members become obedient for a price.

7. *Opportunism — Several styles are used interchangeably, depending on the person involved.* Typically this is seen by 5,5 behavior toward peers, 9,1 behavior toward subordinates, and 1,9 behavior toward those in authority.

The motives are to be on top, number one, but the objectives are self-oriented rather than organizationally productive. Empire building, career enhancement, and similar individual interests take precedence over team results.

A Framework for Studying Performance

The framework of the Teamwork Grid® makes it possible to identify team culture and its impact on performance. Two dimensions of teamwork significantly influence participation: the exercise of power and authority and norms and standards.

Several other dimensions of teamwork also affect participation, but to a large extent these emerge from the way power and authority are exercised and from the way norms and standards regulate. These dimensions include:

- Goals and objectives, the near- and long-term purposes of a team's many activities
- Structure and differentiation, the way job responsibilities are divided and coordinated to achieve the team's objectives
- Feedback and critique, the review and study of team performance
- Morale and cohesion, the emotions and feelings about belonging to the team and the spirit and willingness to help it achieve its ends.

All dimensions must be dealt with to effect comprehensive change and heightened participation.

The Teamwork Grid® permits a common set of signals. Human behavior is complex. Teamwork has many factors influencing the outcome. Each member brings to the team a set of personal assumptions about how to work with others. Possible personal motivations include assumptions about how to be effective, how to avoid failure, how to be liked, how to survive, how to gain approval, and so on.

These personal outlooks are influenced by the team culture which may support some motivations or be adverse to others. The most powerful factors impacting on personal assumptions are the ways in which power and authority are utilized and the ways in which norms develop to control what becomes acceptable and expected behavior of members.

When personal values are incongruent with team values, turnover and dissatisfaction of members occur. When team culture and personal values are in harmony, team members are likely to be satisfied and desire to remain with the organization. This latter condition may be sound or unsound from the point of view of productivity, creativity, and satisfaction — the collective results of team effort.

The Teamwork Grid® provides a framework of reference to locate and thereby define team culture in terms of how power and authority are exercised and the prevailing shared set of norms and standards.

The use of the Teamwork Grid® framework to describe team action has several advantages. It enables a team to locate and define its present culture; it also enables a team to locate and define an ideal to which it can subscribe. A shared vision of the possibilities liberates individual motivations, particularly when the consequences of each cultural location and definition are brought into focus for their impact on productivity, creativity, and satisfaction.

Team culture tends to be most apparent when teamwork action is undertaken. Action dimensions of teamwork — such as setting goals, dividing tasks, or engaging in critique — bring results, good or bad, that reflect the attributes of team culture. When a consistency in behavior is present, the results of teamwork will validate the cultural Teamwork Grid® position of the team.

As with the notion of team culture, there are many physical analogies that can only be demonstrated when action is present. For example, viscosity is a property of fluids that can only be measured and evaluated when velocity or movement occurs. Mass is a property of matter that presents itself when displacement of a medium can be measured. The consequences of action are used to evaluate the property. So too in teamwork, the actions undertaken and their consequences are essential to define the properties of the culture. And the Teamwork Grid® provides a scale of measure that can be shared among team members as a signal system, much as a series of plays for concerted action is used by a sports team.

In summary, we have these relationships:

- A set of individual assumptions shaped by the team culture
- A team culture that provides a limiting or liberating environment
- A set of teamwork action dimensions that reflect the character and definition of the culture
- A set of teamwork results variables expressed in terms of productivity, creativity, and satisfaction

How does participation fit into this model? Participation is the key. Plural effort requires it. Without it, resources of knowledge, skills, and creativity go untapped; synergy becomes impossible; productivity, creativity, and satisfaction are inhibited without it — for the team and for the members.

Team culture may encourage or discourage participation. Its emergence can shape the same culture that set its limits. Finally, participation is the overall energy underlying teamwork.

As team members assess the need for change in their culture, at least two participation requirements come into play: (1) the improvement of individual skills of participation so that team members have self-directed standards of quality and quantity; and (2) a mechanism for change from the current level of quality and quantity of participation to a new and more effective level.

The Teamwork Grid® framework permits examination of teamwork dimensions and evaluation of how they are affected by the team culture. Team building, described in Chapter 11, provides a mechanism for change.

Teamwork Dimensions

In a 9,1 team culture the exercise of power and authority is most often characterized by edicts from the boss. People are held to the line and expected to comply.

Goals and objectives are established by the boss with little or no consultation. The norms and standards are primarily a reflection of the boss's (1) attitude toward the team's performance, and (2) definition of acceptable behavior. Jobs are assigned by the boss. They preserve rigid lines of authority and keep the need for coordination among members to a minimum.

Critique and feedback consist mostly of faultfinding and criticism when things do not go well. Morale and cohesion are low. Frequently there is antagonism toward the organization with feelings of hopelessness that constructive change will occur.

Alan's team has developed a 9,1 culture. Several team members share strong 9,1 orientations; thus power and authority are not clearly delineated and team action closely resembles a power struggle resulting in an ongoing series of win–lose exchanges with selfish goals and objectives substituted for those of the team. Norms and standards are unlikely to be uniform except for a shared willingness to engage in win–lose fighting to resolve differences. There is likely to be a high degree of concern for territorial rights and low cooperation among members. Blame placing and defensiveness characterize feedback. Morale is low; members are resigned to their situation or contemplating leaving to escape it.

Diagnosis of Teamwork

The following statements and scales should assist you in determining the extent to which your own team contains elements of the 9,1 culture. Rate the statements from 1 (uncharacteristic) to 9 (highly characteristic) to describe your team.

1. Directions: Directions come from the boss; even though these may be resisted, few efforts to change them succeed.

1	2	3	4	5	6	7	8	9
Completely uncharacteristic				Partially characteristic			Highly characteristic	

2. Meetings: A top-down approach predetermines meeting agenda. Team members offer information when requested; otherwise, acceptance of topics is more or less passive or else actively resisted.

1	2	3	4	5	6	7	8	9

Completely uncharacteristic   Partially characteristic   Highly characteristic

3. Conflict: Rank is used to cut off conflict and to decide between conflicting viewpoints; the disagreement goes underground.

1	2	3	4	5	6	7	8	9

Completely uncharacteristic   Partially characteristic   Highly characteristic

4. Objectives: Objectives for results which are imposed are considered to be final.

1	2	3	4	5	6	7	8	9

Completely uncharacteristic   Partially characteristic   Highly characteristic

5. Innovation: Suggestions or novel ideas are resisted and the resistance is overcome only through persistent effort, if at all.

1	2	3	4	5	6	7	8	9

Completely uncharacteristic   Partially characteristic   Highly characteristic

6. Communication (candor): Communication is chiefly in the form of directives on a need-to-know basis; other than reporting, little information is sought from members or others.

1	2	3	4	5	6	7	8	9
Completely uncharacteristic				Partially characteristic				Highly characteristic

7. Job descriptions: Job responsibilities are compartmentalized; coordination among members is mostly through the formal chain of command.

1	2	3	4	5	6	7	8	9
Completely uncharacteristic				Partially characteristic				Highly characteristic

8. Delegation: Members have minimum latitude in carrying out their assignments; they are told what to do—not why.

1	2	3	4	5	6	7	8	9
Completely uncharacteristic				Partially characteristic				Highly characteristic

9. Quality: Highest quality standards are emphasized; methods used to get them are not as important.

1	2	3	4	5	6	7	8	9
Completely uncharacteristic				Partially characteristic				Highly characteristic

10. Performance appraisals: Performance reviews are centered on weaknesses and failures to measure up, emphasized at the expense of evaluating achievements.

1	2	3	4	5	6	7	8	9
Completely uncharacteristic				Partially characteristic				Highly characteristic

11. Team spirit: Members are more concerned with self-preservation and protecting their own turf than with team-wide activities.

1	2	3	4	5	6	7	8	9
Completely uncharacteristic				Partially characteristic				Highly characteristic

12. Commitment: Members are guided more by fear of being seen as disloyal or insubordinate than by team-centered loyalty and commitment.

1	2	3	4	5	6	7	8	9
Completely uncharacteristic				Partially characteristic				Highly characteristic

In the following chart total your ratings for each scale.* Transfer your total to the 9,1 column in Figure 9.1. An interpretation of the numbers is provided in Chapter 9.

Scale	Rating
1. Directions	
2. Meetings	
3. Conflict	
4. Objectives	
5. Innovation	
6. Communication	
7. Job descriptions	
8. Delegation	
9. Quality	
10. Performance appraisals	
11. Team spirit	
12. Commitment	
Total	

*Maximum total possible is 108; minimum total possible is 12.

Chapter Three

Three Strikes and You're Out

Coordinating Effort Towards the Common Goal

Ian Brenner, marketing director at the Congress Hotel, was anxious as he walked toward the executive offices. Bill Herzog, the general manager, had asked to see him on rather short notice. Ian could not imagine why Bill wanted to see him. After Ian entered the office, the two men exchanged "good mornings" and sat down.

BILL: Ian, I've brought you in to talk about my concern with the marketing group you're running. I've really been puzzled about what's wrong and I've come to a conclusion.

Ian shifted uneasily in his chair and said:

IAN: What's wrong? I thought we were the top group in the eastern region. We've been pulling the departments together and complementing each one. I don't think you ever had teamwork like this. I sure think it's a new world here since Steve left. He was on everybody's hit list. It really worries me that you think something's wrong.

BILL: Well, I didn't expect this to be easy. Let's think about some of the results.

The older, gray-haired man turned to the window and watched the steady stream of morning traffic. He took out his pipe, looked at it, and set it into a big bronze ashtray.

BILL: You see those cars? There are about six percent fewer that stop here than two years ago.

IAN: Well, you're right, but it takes time for this to come together, Bill.

BILL: We've talked about that before too, Ian. The regional manager has taken note and he's not happy.

IAN: Look, Bill, you know the troubles we had when Steve was here. I moved in here with three new people and I said to myself, "I'm going to make this THE place to work." We attracted four of the brightest graduates of Case and made a team.

BILL: Yes, I have separation notices from two of them. Human resources gave them to me yesterday. That's what convinced me not to put off this talk. You know what they said as their reason for leaving? Words like "stifled," "nonproductive," "pacifying." You've seen their notices. What did they mean to you?

IAN: I don't know. Young people are not the same anymore. Everybody's got an itch to be general manager overnight. We've got a team. You're just bound to have some mavericks.

BILL: Tell me about your team.

Ian shifted, took a swallow of coffee and set the fine china cup carefully into the saucer. At times like these he wished he smoked a pipe. It gave one more time to think about a reply.

IAN: Well, you know that when I came here the marketing department was a one-man show. I knew Peter and Rod from college and I thought we could work well together. Nick was Rod's roommate at Hotel School at Cornell. We sat down and decided we could smooth out the agony if we held regular meetings with the other departments. There was a lot of strife then, you remember? Rod had the idea we should get away from the scene of the battle so he set up our Tuesday sessions at Le Club.

Peter had the idea that we could work together better if we had some social time together. Remember? He put out the proposal for the softball league — Congress uniforms, the whole thing for less than $7000.

We fit together like part of a puzzle. All of us — well, except for the two rebels that just quit. I'd say it was no big loss. Right at the start we set out goals to bring the departments together. We opened up their ideas and implemented most of them. You remember Charlie Shaver had the idea of menu simplification. He was having trouble with the kitchen service and he suggested reducing the menu selection to six items. That saved us a lot of service complaints.

BILL: Yeah, that solved the kitchen service problem, but our prime restaurant turnover fell.

IAN: That wasn't our fault. The new Rosemont property opened and it drew away some of our business. We did everything we could.

BILL: I don't know. Have you ever thought that, in obliging Charlie, you disobliged the customer? Our dinner clientele are increasingly sophisticated. They want an interesting menu selection and they want no lapses in the service.

IAN: We pulled together really well to solve that one. We reviewed that from end to end and we couldn't find a single misstep.

BILL: Ian, I don't think we solved it. We lost turnover. We oiled the waters, but that wasn't good enough. Go on about your team.

Ian was increasingly uncomfortable. He was on the hot seat and he didn't like being disliked. He continued, though:

IAN: I don't know. You know the good we've done. The departments are speaking to each other. We put oil where Steve put sand.

BILL: Ian, they are speaking to each other, and you know what they're saying? They're saying that we've lost our competitive edge. Everyone's happy as hell, but our market share is falling. And they are losing confidence in marketing.

IAN: We have good teamwork.

BILL: And two-hour coffee klatches. Ian, Ian, face up! You and your group are soft and self-indulgent. You had good ideas when you were at Dayton. You were highly recommended. But you've gone slushy and we can't afford it. You've surrounded yourself with yes-men.

IAN: I don't like what's happening.

BILL: Neither do I. It has gone too far. Ian, I'm putting you on notice. You have two months in which to give me evidence that this hotel is back in the running. We can no longer afford sports promotion and good fellowship as the principal contribution of your team. It's time for results. I'll expect a progress report from you every two weeks for the next two months.

I'll make a judgment from the condition of the bottom line. Unless the erosion of our share and the decline of our profits is at least stabilized by that time, you'll have to seek your fortune somewhere else.

Ian's overriding concern was to be well-liked. The power and authority he needs to exert for direction and coordination is subordinated to his interest in smoothing out conflicts that may threaten the friendly atmosphere he wishes to maintain. When Ian brags about the marketing group's good "teamwork" with the other divisions, he is referring to an absence of tensions rather than a coordinated effort toward a common task.

The two "mavericks" who quit were rejected by the team for their efforts at sound problem solving which threatened the friendly, easygoing atmosphere. After they announced their resignations Ian concluded that they were "no big loss," thus isolating himself from them.

Ian appeared completely surprised at Bill's negative assessment of his team's performance. Ian and the team do not seek accurate critique and feedback. When it is presented to them, they behave defensively, as shown when Ian was confronted by Bill with facts that contradicted his rosy view. Because they cannot bring themselves to face the objective data on their performance, they are completely unable to plan strategically for achieving high-level results.

Teamwork Dimensions

As expressed by the Teamwork Grid® discussed in Chapter 2, Ian's team has a 1,9 team culture. In the 1,9 exercise of power and authority, the boss is likely to be a friend rather than a leader. Subordinates are thought of as friends. Such a boss may mask his or her power and authority by broadcasting warmth and encouragement and avoiding controversial issues that may generate conflict and cause bad feelings.

Goals and objectives are geared toward keeping individuals well-related and harmonious rather than toward the productive purposes of the team. However, the team is likely to be satisfied with its accomplishments.

Norms and standards in a 1,9 culture permit the satisfaction, personal convenience, and whims of team members to prevail over issues of productivity that would interfere with these concerns. Such standards often prevail when it seems easier to tolerate ineffective actions than to confront people about shortcomings.

In the 1,9 team, job assignments are based on expressed personal preferences rather than demonstrated competence. Congeniality is also an important factor in settling the issue of who works with whom.

Critique and feedback are concerned with emphasizing positive aspects of performance while downplaying or ignoring problems. Morale is generally high, but it comes from a sense of team members being well-related to one another rather than from positive feelings that come from true accomplishment or performance.

Diagnosis of Teamwork

The following statements and scales will assist you in determining the extent to which your own team contains elements of the 1,9 culture. Rate the statements from 1 (uncharacteristic) to 9 (highly characteristic) as a description of your team.

1. Directions: Suggestions keep work moving with the least friction among members; individual responsibilities are minimized and put in general terms that do not create pressure.

1	2	3	4	5	6	7	8	9
Completely uncharacteristic				Partially characteristic				Highly characteristic

2. Meetings: Discussion centers on personal concerns more than on team-centered issues.

1	2	3	4	5	6	7	8	9

Completely uncharacteristic   Partially characteristic   Highly characteristic

3. Conflict: When conflict arises members step in to soothe feelings and bring parties together.

1	2	3	4	5	6	7	8	9

Completely uncharacteristic   Partially characteristic   Highly characteristic

4. Objectives: More concern is placed on what members think and want than on achieving high performance objectives for the team.

1	2	3	4	5	6	7	8	9

Completely uncharacteristic   Partially characteristic   Highly characteristic

5. Innovation: Acceptance of ideas is intended to convey appreciation and support; whether or not they are relevant is secondary.

1	2	3	4	5	6	7	8	9

Completely uncharacteristic   Partially characteristic   Highly characteristic

6. Communication (candor): Social and nonwork topics make the day pleasant; discussion of work is incidental.

1	2	3	4	5	6	7	8	9

Completely
uncharacteristic

Partially
characteristic

Highly
characteristic

7. Job descriptions: Members are encouraged to interpret their responsibilities in ways that please them.

1	2	3	4	5	6	7	8	9

Completely
uncharacteristic

Partially
characteristic

Highly
characteristic

8. Delegation: Projects are implemented on the basis of what each member prefers to do rather than competence, time available, or priority relative to other tasks.

1	2	3	4	5	6	7	8	9

Completely
uncharacteristic

Partially
characteristic

Highly
characteristic

9. Quality: Standards of quality receive lip service but do not affect members' decisions or actions; gaining and maintaining approval of other members is more important.

1	2	3	4	5	6	7	8	9

Completely
uncharacteristic

Partially
characteristic

Highly
characteristic

10. Performance appraisals: Performance appraisals are marked by compliments and positive affirmation with mistakes and errors rarely discussed.

1	2	3	4	5	6	7	8	9
Completely uncharacteristic			Partially characteristic			Highly characteristic		

11. Team spirit: Interactions are warm and friendly but this contributes little to strengthened performance.

1	2	3	4	5	6	7	8	9
Completely uncharacteristic			Partially characteristic			Highly characteristic		

12. Commitment: Commitment is from appreciation of the human relations made possible through work.

1	2	3	4	5	6	7	8	9
Completely uncharacteristic			Partially characteristic			Highly characteristic		

In the following chart total your ratings for each scale.*
Transfer your total to the 1,9 column in Figure 9.1. An interpretation of the numbers is provided in Chapter 9.

Scale	Rating
1. Directions	
2. Meetings	
3. Conflict	
4. Objectives	
5. Innovation	
6. Communication	
7. Job descriptions	
8. Delegation	
9. Quality	
10. Performance appraisals	
11. Team spirit	
12. Commitment	
Total	

*Maximum total possible is 108; minimum total possible is 12.

Chapter Four

Father Knows Best

Developing Mutual Feedback and Critique

T he wave broke gently on the beach and retreated in fin-
gers of white foam. The lights of the city shone in narrow
rippling paths across the black waters of the sound. On the
horizon a new moon stood poised, a little big for its age.
Jerry Hunt and Art Myers came to a halt near the water's
edge. They are project managers in the industrial goods marketing department of a glass products company.

Jerry reached out and pulled his jogging shoes a little closer
to where his bare heels dug holes in the sand. Art sat beside
him. Finally, Jerry broke the silence.

JERRY: The tide's rising. If you were a shell on the beach,
you'd be covered by now. What's happened to you?
Where's all that zip and enthusiasm? Lately you've been
awfully quiet and closed, especially at work.

ART: I'm in a survival mode these days. Since Peg got tossed
out of her job, we've become a one-income couple and the
good life runs high. I've got two choices — do things the
company way or lose the apartment. Neither one suits me
very well.

JERRY: Yeah, you've never been one for letting someone else
do your thinking.

Art hugged his knees closer against the chill of the night
air. His T-shirt felt clammy from the perspiration of his run.

ART: Jerry, you and I joined the company with stars in our
eyes. But the last year or two, this operation got to me.
We're contaminated. We can't afford to leave and it's stifling us. Oh, the money's good — too good. We're hooked.
I used to dream about independence when I was a kid. It's
the same now. Only instead of my own father, I've got

Charlie and others up the line in the company, all giving me orders, all requiring obedience and giving rewards when I'm a good boy. You've bought into the system and you're one of *them*. I haven't, and I'm uncomfortable.

JERRY: Sure I have and it's not that bad. I can't believe you feel this way.

ART: Jerry, I like to contribute. I'm not afraid of work. I often work all night. But there's a mantle of control. We salute the boss, follow orders, but they're *his* orders. He defines the work, sets the schedules — all down to the last detail. There's a culture here. We all follow it and nobody better break ranks.

JERRY: It's the same everywhere!

ART: No, it isn't. What about Bob Saunders? His department hums and it has got some freedom. Bob's not the strongest guy in the world, but his place turns out the best work. It's always on top. You know, it's a little pocket of excellence in that great big overgrown family tree of a corporation.

JERRY: Why don't you put in for a transfer?

ART: I have. But there's a lineup. Charlie can't figure out why so many want into consumer marketing.

JERRY: It'd be a good move for you. But why not try to make our department another — what did you call it? — pocket of excellence?

ART: I've thought about that. I talked to Charlie. He couldn't understand what I meant. You know, I think everyone here has just bought in. They do their job, get paid for it, and spend their spare time thinking about the next long weekend. They've got a social schedule like you wouldn't believe. I don't know how they do so much in a few days.

JERRY: They get their kicks out of the world.

ART: Well, I'm out of step. I get a real bang out of doing good stuff. I want to be a part of something good. I didn't spend those six years in college for this!

JERRY: The guys won't change.

ART: No, never. They're in lockstep and the company is a means to an end. Charlie thought I was crazy. Damn.

Two weeks passed and Art and Jerry are attending a monthly department meeting being conducted by their boss, Charlie Coleman.

Charlie drew a broken line on the sheet with a wax pencil to extrapolate the sales trend. It was downward at an angle of about 15 degrees. He ended his report with the words, "and that's the way I see it. Could we have the lights please? Let's take a coffee break and then I'll detail what the action plan is and what steps each of us need to take."

The fluorescent lights broke the darkness of the conference room, not all at once but irregularly in small sets of random sequence. Art Myers thought to himself, "The command is given and we all fall into line — each at his own pace but finally all in line. I'm the holdout but I come on line too. It's the voltage of the command."

The industrial goods marketing group gathered around the coffee cart. Charlie Coleman held back a smile as his flock helped themselves to the refreshments. Talk was light and cheerful and not about business or the presentation just made. Each manager was waiting to hear his part in Charlie's game plan.

Only Art held back. He had not left his conference seat. He was busy drawing a small logic diagram with boxes labeled "position audit," "trends and forecasts," "assumptions," "strengths," and "weaknesses." He listed a set of points beside each box.

Charlie was listening to Jerry Hunt's compliments on the presentation. The pleasant syrup of Jerry's praise reinforced his good feelings. As he observed Art, his warmth faded. He frowned, partly because he disliked a straggler in his command and partly because he chafed at Art's challenge to his own clear action plan. He liked Art; his work was always first-class — well-ordered and logical. Still, Art was a maverick — always challenging, always out of step.

Charlie wished Bob Saunders had an opening. Art would fit in better there. He would miss the quality work, but the burr would be gone from under the saddle.

Charlie walked over to Art. "How about coffee and a danish before the next call to order?"

Art started to explain his analysis, but Charlie brushed it aside, "Not now. I've got the plan pretty well worked out. Come on over, join the party. Besides, I want to hear about Peg's new challenge as a homemaker."

Art sighed, disappointed at the lack of interest. But Charlie was a personable and commanding boss. Art got up reluctantly and joined the group, feeling a little awkward that he had no big weekend to conjure up into tall tales like the others.

About 10 minutes later Charlie gathered the clan and resumed the meeting. Flipping the pages of the chart, he gave out the work assignments.

Art spoke up, "We haven't spent time on the analysis yet. Don't you think we should pool our views on the problem before jumping to conclusions?"

There was silence as the idea set in. Charlie looked at his watch, frowned, and considered Art's suggestions. "We've got a little over an hour to set this. I'll tell you what. We can take, say, 20 minutes to develop individual views, present them for, say, 5 minutes each, then discuss and conclude. We've got to leave here with an action plan."

Jerry Hunt spoke up. "Look, Charlie, it's Art who wants all this. I'd just as soon get at your plan. You're the boss around here. Why should we waste your time?"

The group talked together for about 5 minutes, ending in a decision to hear Art out. Charlie kept firm control, happy that Jerry's intervention kept him from being too heavy, happy that he didn't have to listen to a lot of divergent views.

By now Art was odd man out. Nonetheless, he took the floor and presented his position. Although the presentation was crisp and logical, Charlie nitpicked every step. It would take more research and more thinking.

Someone started to offer support for Art's idea when Charlie intervened, "Look, you guys, I know you all have appointments at noon — squash, lunch, jogging. If we look at my plan now, we have a good chance of getting out of here on time."

Jerry Hunt gave his usual "confidence in the leader" routine and all eyes turned to Charlie's work plan. Charlie had set out the detail well, all neat little boxes of work with due dates and responsibilities.

At one point Art intervened, saying, "Charlie, how come you can make sweeping judgments and I have to justify every little step?" Charlie only frowned and continued.

It was 10 minutes to 12:00 when they pushed back their chairs and left, each hurrying to their noon appointments — all but Art, who sat alone.

The department meeting and Art Myer's performance had weighed heavily on Charlie Coleman's mind. After considering it for several days, he asked for a meeting with the company's human resources director.

Joe Forrest waved jauntily to the marketing office secretaries as he pushed open the heavy oak door of Charlie Coleman's office.

"You called, master?"

Charlie Coleman was hunched over a computer printout. He grinned broadly as he recognized the human resources director.

Joe plopped down into one of the modern armchairs opposite Charlie.

"What's on your mind?" Joe asked.

Charlie pursed his lips and rubbed his temples as he gathered his thoughts.

CHARLIE: Myers.

JOE: Art Myers? Your wonder boy?

CHARLIE: Yeah, Art Myers. But I think I'd call him my delinquent wonder boy. I'm having trouble with him, Joe. He marches to a different drummer, and I'm getting fed up. His work is good but he's a disruption to the smooth working of my department.

JOE: How's that?

CHARLIE: He balks at every direction. Always wants to set out some course of his own.

JOE: Is his thinking wrong?

CHARLIE: No. Not wrong. Deviant. He just doesn't go along with my direction. He's got good ideas, yes. But I can't afford to incorporate his logic in every move I take. I want to set out the work and have it done. No ifs, ands, or buts. I'm running this department and I want loyalty, not questions. That's the way this company was built and that's the way I want my department run.

Joe thought for a minute and then said:

JOE: Myers has been pushing for a transfer to Bob Saunder's group. He's not happy either. But I don't think we can accommodate that for some time. Looks like you'll have to live with him a while.

CHARLIE: Look, Joe, I've got a big happy family here. Myers is a pain in the you-know-what. I've tried everything. A transfer is the only answer.

JOE: What have you tried?

CHARLIE: I've counseled; I've reasoned. I've promised him key projects if he can do what he's now doing without so much fuss. I gave him a small raise at mid-year. One night I took him out to dinner for a heart-to-heart talk.

JOE: How did the conversation go?

CHARLIE: Waste of time. I told him what I expected. He was like one of those kewpie dolls on a spring — bounced back every time I hit him.

Look, I want to find an answer. Where did this idiot get the idea of critique anyway? He's always asking for a critique of the meetings and everything else. I let him do it one day and I damn near died. He talked about creative leg room and contribution and pleasure of accomplishment. As I said, he marches to a different drummer, Joe. And he spooks the other guys. He's friends with Jerry Hunt and he upsets Jerry all the time. Jerry gives me support and appreciates the direction I give. I tell you something's got to be done.

Come on, Joe. Help me. I've tried everything. I can't fire him. I've got no cause. But I don't want him.

JOE: Charlie, he's really a gem. And besides, he's stable. You've got a high turnover. Build on Art.

CHARLIE: No! Figure something else out!

Joe thought a minute, then said:

JOE: Special Applications. We've got a retirement next month. We can really use someone with a lot of energy there. It's not as sophisticated as this operation but it's a good opportunity for someone who likes a challenge. Do you think he'll move?

CHARLIE: Take him.

JOE: I'll see what I can do. I'll let you know the end of the week.

CHARLIE: Thank you very much.

Charlie's number one priority is loyalty and obedience from his team members. This locks up the team's creativity and productivity in a vise grip. Under these circumstances, excellence is rarely possible.

The rewards for compliance as a member of this team come in the form of praise from the boss, vacations, and pay incentives. Art observes that compliance in exchange for these rewards is the value most shared by the members: "If you've bought into the system, you're one of THEM." Team members do not rock the boat.

Art feels like an outsider because he exerts independent initiative toward solving problems in the team. Art's questions and comments about Charlie's plan at the meeting are met with impatience because objective feedback and critique are not welcome in a paternalistically run team. Members of the team stand by Charlie in resisting candid feedback because any open discussion might be seen as a threat to Charlie's authority — and a threat to the team's hidden agreement for gaining rewards through compliance. In such an atmosphere objective data, including the attitudes and feelings of members, are not available to be applied to the problems and tasks at hand unless it comes directly from the boss.

Teamwork Dimensions

In a paternalistic team culture power and authority are firmly vested in the boss. The goals and objectives of the team are those of the boss. People are expected to comply, and they are shown appreciation when they do. The accepted ways of operating are derivations of the overall norms and standards of loyalty and compliance.

Job assignments both ensure the boss's direction and control and heighten the members' dependence on the boss. Compliance with an unattractive assignment is often rewarded with a more attractive one.

Feedback and critique only flow from the boss down. Subordinates are complimented for compliance and reprimanded when compliance is not forthcoming. Feedback directed toward the boss is viewed as undermining proper authority and is discouraged. For those team members content to go along for the benefits compliance can bring, morale can be high, particularly during periods of success. However, members can become frustrated under this culture when they want to try new and different ways of operating without being seen as disloyal.

Diagnosis of Teamwork

The following statements and scales will assist you in determining the extent to which your own team contains elements of a paternalistic culture. Rate the statements from 1 (uncharacteristic) to 9 (highly characteristic) as a description of your team.

1. Directions: The boss determines the activities to be accomplished and how they are to be done; team members are treated well and compliance is expected in everyone's best interest.

1	2	3	4	5	6	7	8	9
Completely uncharacteristic				Partially characteristic				Highly characteristic

2. Meetings: Out of a desire to please and to avoid reprimand, members confine their participation to the boss-determined topics, rarely introducing other topics.

1	2	3	4	5	6	7	8	9
Completely uncharacteristic				Partially characteristic				Highly characteristic

3. Conflict: While members are thanked for expressing differing viewpoints, conflict is viewed as disruptive and terminated by the boss at the earliest opportunity.

1	2	3	4	5	6	7	8	9

Completely
uncharacteristic

Partially
characteristic

Highly
characteristic

4. Objectives: Members are expected to accept enthusiastically the objectives assigned them.

1	2	3	4	5	6	7	8	9

Completely
uncharacteristic

Partially
characteristic

Highly
characteristic

5. Innovation: A positive attitude exists toward innovation but new ideas are not really welcomed.

1	2	3	4	5	6	7	8	9

Completely
uncharacteristic

Partially
characteristic

Highly
characteristic

6. Communication (candor): Members are told what to do but in ways that encourage their acquiescence.

1	2	3	4	5	6	7	8	9

Completely
uncharacteristic

Partially
characteristic

Highly
characteristic

7. Job descriptions: Responsibilities are outlined by the boss to ensure control; team members frequently seek guidance even though it's not really needed.

1	2	3	4	5	6	7	8	9

Completely uncharacteristic   Partially characteristic   Highly characteristic

8. Delegation: The autonomy granted members is reduced when they fail to meet expectations.

1	2	3	4	5	6	7	8	9

Completely uncharacteristic   Partially characteristic   Highly characteristic

9. Quality: Quality standards are primarily a reflection of what the boss expects, and team members usually comply as directed.

1	2	3	4	5	6	7	8	9

Completely uncharacteristic   Partially characteristic   Highly characteristic

10. Performance appraisals: Performance reviews are characterized by praise for compliance with directives and admonishments for shortcomings, but with the promise of restored good feelings when shortcomings have been corrected.

1	2	3	4	5	6	7	8	9

Completely uncharacteristic   Partially characteristic   Highly characteristic

11. Team spirit: Coordination is ensured by the boss who encourages team members to accept what is asked of them in a loyal way and without complaints.

1	2	3	4	5	6	7	8	9
Completely uncharacteristic				Partially characteristic				Highly characteristic

12. Commitment: When members discharge their duties and obligations as expected of them, they are taken care of in a positive manner which contributes to their feelings of security.

1	2	3	4	5	6	7	8	9
Completely uncharacteristic				Partially characteristic				Highly characteristic

In the following chart total your ratings for each scale.* Transfer your total to the Paternalism column in Figure 9.1. An interpretation of the numbers is provided in Chapter 9.

Scale	Rating
1. Directions	
2. Meetings	
3. Conflict	
4. Objectives	
5. Innovation	
6. Communication	
7. Job descriptions	
8. Delegation	
9. Quality	
10. Performance appraisals	
11. Team spirit	
12. Commitment	
Total	

*Maximum total possible is 108; minimum total possible is 12.

Chapter Five

Living in the Past

Building Morale That Counts

The racing tires squealed as the BMW swung into the driveway at 6:30. Samantha James reached into the backseat to recover her slim brown attaché case. As she passed her husband Rod's car in the driveway, she noted that the hood was almost cold. Rod is a senior contracts administrator for a large federal agency and Samantha works for a public relations firm. Before his present job assignment Rod had enjoyed his association with a government agency and found the work interesting and worthwhile. Lately, however, Samantha had noticed a change.

"Early quitting time again," she thought and waved at her husband who was standing at the picture window, a martini in his hand. She pushed open the front door and dropped her keys on the hall table.

"Bad day at the office, dear?" she asked, as she noted the level of the glass martini pitcher; its sides were frosted halfway up.

"I made us a drink," Rod grinned.

"You made *you* a drink, old buddy. I've got work to do tonight. I'll settle for a Perrier with a touch of lemon. Want to get it or shall I?"

"No trouble."

As Rod headed through the swinging doors of the kitchen, she thought about her exciting day. Two contracts successfully closed and a good start on the new marketing strategy. Rod returned.

ROD: I set out the new plants you bought last week. It was a nice relief to dig in the earth. That job of mine leaves me cold. I wish I was into something exciting, like you.

SAMANTHA: You make your own excitement, Rod — at least that's what my boss preaches. He's really a good leader.

Draws us all out. Makes it challenging and fun. He challenges a lot, but that's what keeps it interesting.

ROD: Sam, I'm really worried.

Rod fingered the ice in his martini, fished out the lemon slice, and took a long sip. The grandfather clock struck the half-hour, 6:30. He had left work at 4:45 and beaten the rush hour. It was a long drive and the traffic could double his travel time. He got up and stood at the French doors, watching the sun set on his world. "A good world," he thought. "Two nice cars in the driveway. Well, at least one. The wagon was a bit tired. If you opened a can of rust remover, it would disappear. Gotta do something one of these days. Still, it is a good world." The new plantings were taking nicely, and the bright green of the new growth haloed the winter kill.

Sam got up, put her hand on her husband's shoulder, and quietly spoke. "Rod, you take things too hard. You're a real worrywart. Come on and sit down. Tell me about it and you'll feel better."

ROD: I don't know where to start.

SAMANTHA: Try the beginning.

ROD: Well, in the beginning, God created . . .

SAMANTHA: Not that far back.

Rod grinned at his joke, pushed a stray lock of hair off his forehead, glanced at his nails, and began.

ROD: Today, we had a pep talk. First quarter results. The agency director himself came down from Washington. He wasn't happy.

SAMANTHA: What were the results?

ROD: Productivity off four percent. Complaints up. Costs about double. Labor negotiations are just starting and the employees' association wants the world.

SAMANTHA: Sounds bad. What does he want you guys to do? Pull a miracle?

ROD: He didn't say. He was just awfully critical and unhappy. You know how the agency is.

SAMANTHA: Why don't you quit and get these people off your back? You could find something else. Leave the problems with Jerry and the rest. After all, Jerry's the boss; he's responsible. I have my job.

ROD: That's no answer. There are too many benefits and we need a double income. It wouldn't be easy to find a job, and I certainly would miss the guys. It would be a big step.

SAMANTHA: What's so good about it — the belonging, I mean?

ROD: Well, for one thing, it's really a good job. Jerry doesn't ask for much and our team works pretty well independently.

SAMANTHA: Do you ever get together and talk about it?

ROD: No, we just work alone. After all, the program director sets out the major plans and objectives.

SAMANTHA: Does Jerry add much?

ROD: No, he used to try, but we're not really team players. It wastes a lot of time. We look after our own areas and keep a keen eye on what the latest message is.

SAMANTHA: But it doesn't sound like it's working.

ROD: Well, we've survived two years since we reorganized the region.

SAMANTHA: Don't you have objectives, or management by objectives, or anything like that?

ROD: Jerry started that last year. The agency had a big push on MBO. Each of us set some goals — mostly to hold our own. It's a tough position we're in. Staying where you are is like running up the down escalator.

SAMANTHA: What happened?

ROD: Well, it was a dud of an effort. The objectives bounced back and forth three or four times, but the agency wouldn't accept them. Jerry got called in once. In the end, they gave us general guidelines for what they wanted and we filled in numbers we thought they would accept.

SAMANTHA: Did Jerry critique that way of arriving at objectives?

ROD: Heavens, no! We were all fed up. He gave us the message and we followed the guidelines to the letter. I think the director's strategy is to raise the performance standards bit by bit and let the separate departments worry about details.

SAMANTHA: So it's survival against the agency?

ROD: That's about it. I hadn't thought about it before, but we do try to keep a low profile.

SAMANTHA: How's that?

ROD: Well, we accept orders and do our best to keep the region from coming in last when the performance statistics are announced. That would draw attention.

SAMANTHA: Shouldn't it be one of the best? It has got the newest processing equipment. The start-up team left it in good shape, didn't they? After all, they were there more than three months longer than they were supposed to be.

ROD: Dammit, Sam, you know that things go wrong. It's Murphy's Law. Sure they did a job, but they left problems. They should have left it with nothing to do but push the button in the morning and shut it down in the evening. None of us were satisfied to see them go, but they twisted our arms for sign off.

Samantha sensed Rod's irritation and changed the topic — unfortunately back to MBO.

SAMANTHA: When you had the big push on MBO, did you get together to set out how you'd achieve the objective — help each other and all that?

ROD: Look, Sam, it's not in our makeup to do that. Jerry wanted to and he got us together. We sat around with great gobs of silence while Jerry pushed. It was like trying to get volunteers for a fund-raising drive. We all know our jobs and we do them. That's the best way. I don't want to work all night like Bill Johnston.

SAMANTHA: You know, maybe it's what *you* have to do.

ROD: You know, when I was deputy area manager, I had some spirit. Remember? I used to work hard, bring stuff home. I wish I was back there. We worked together, set objectives, tried and failed, tried again, pushed it through. That was excitement. I'd almost forgotten. I've gone numb here. By damn, it's been a long time since I had any spirit!

You know, I think I've got a copy of the employee association proposal in the car. I'm going to get it and do a little work tonight. I'm going to talk with Jerry tomorrow. I think something can be done. The guys will sure resist.

Sam nodded as she saw the light in his eyes and the smile on his lips. She rose, smoothed her skirt, and headed for the kitchen, carrying the remains of the martini pitcher.

This team exerts only the minimal effort required rather than challenging themselves to reach a superlative level of performance. Their only goal is to avoid drawing negative attention to themselves.

They do not formulate their own goals. Instead they simply "fill in the numbers" on prewritten agency objectives so that the task is minimally completed. In reality, it is a meaningless exercise.

Jerry, the boss, exerts very little power and authority, and the other team members follow suit by showing little enthusiasm or initiative for agency projects. The low commitment—and thus low achievement—were reflected in first quarter results reviewed by the agency director.

Morale is low. Such an atmosphere makes it virtually impossible to get top-notch contributions from teammates.

Teamwork Dimensions

In the 1,1 exercise of power and authority, the boss may have little more than a title. Such a boss becomes isolated from daily pressures and exerts little influence on communication, coordination, or decision making. What remains is a vacuum that the team members must fill as they see fit—and low expectations are coupled with low achievement.

In the 1,1 culture goals and objectives are rarely generated. More typically, direction comes from outside the team with the boss passing along the "word" and members responding by meeting the minimum requirements for performance.

Norms and standards (e.g., being late to meetings, being unprepared, or "doing one's own thing") are more likely to have been established by neglect or accident than by intention. As such, standards of performance descend to the lowest levels likely to be tolerated by the organization.

Work assignments are likely to reflect availability rather than talent or competence. Job priorities are only established to relieve pressures fed in from outside the team. Otherwise, members gravitate toward the least demanding tasks.

Feedback and critique are minimal. Shortcomings and problems are ignored unless they have reached serious proportions. Members are expected to look after their own responsibilities, and feedback from others is neither expected nor welcomed. The 1,1 condition of morale and cohesion is often expressed as, "It's no use, nothing can be done anyway." This attitude may result in withdrawal and alienation: people do not want to be involved.

Diagnosis of Teamwork

The following statements and scales will assist you in determining the extent to which your own team contains elements of the 1,1 culture. Rate the statements from 1 (uncharacteristic) to 9 (highly characteristic) as a description of your team.

1. Directions: Directions are minimal; action is based mostly on doing things ritually or one thing at a time as new demands arise.

1	2	3	4	5	6	7	8	9
Completely uncharacteristic				Partially characteristic				Highly characteristic

2. Meetings: Few meetings take place; when they do the exchanges are halfhearted with little give-and-take.

1	2	3	4	5	6	7	8	9

Completely   Partially   Highly
uncharacteristic   characteristic   characteristic

3. Conflict: Members avoid taking positions that provoke conflict or becoming involved in those which exist.

1	2	3	4	5	6	7	8	9

Completely   Partially   Highly
uncharacteristic   characteristic   characteristic

4. Objectives: Members work as they see fit with little examination of objectives or development of expectations for achieving them.

1	2	3	4	5	6	7	8	9

Completely   Partially   Highly
uncharacteristic   characteristic   characteristic

5. Innovation: New ideas are accepted but then are unlikely to be acted on.

1	2	3	4	5	6	7	8	9

Completely   Partially   Highly
uncharacteristic   characteristic   characteristic

6. Communication (candor): Members get the word on a "message-passing" basis; little in-depth discussion of job activities occurs.

1	2	3	4	5	6	7	8	9

Completely   Partially   Highly
uncharacteristic   characteristic   characteristic

7. Job descriptions: Members are unwilling to move beyond narrow interpretations of job descriptions.

1	2	3	4	5	6	7	8	9

Completely uncharacteristic   Partially characteristic   Highly characteristic

8. Delegation: Assignments are not planned; they are handed out to whomever is available.

1	2	3	4	5	6	7	8	9

Completely uncharacteristic   Partially characteristic   Highly characteristic

9. Quality: Quality standards scarcely exist because they have never been established and/or refined.

1	2	3	4	5	6	7	8	9

Completely uncharacteristic   Partially characteristic   Highly characteristic

10. Performance appraisals: Performance appraisals are perfunctory with little effort to dig in to real issues of effectiveness.

1	2	3	4	5	6	7	8	9

Completely uncharacteristic   Partially characteristic   Highly characteristic

11. Team spirit: This is a gathering of individuals and not a team.

1	2	3	4	5	6	7	8	9

Completely   Partially   Highly
uncharacteristic   characteristic   characteristic

12. Commitment: Members stay because of pay and benefits; there is little loyalty to organization success.

1	2	3	4	5	6	7	8	9

Completely   Partially   Highly
uncharacteristic   characteristic   characteristic

In the following chart total your ratings for each scale.* Transfer your total to the 1,1 column in Figure 9.1. An interpretation of the numbers is provided in Chapter 9.

Scale	Rating
1. Directions	
2. Meetings	
3. Conflict	
4. Objectives	
5. Innovation	
6. Communication	
7. Job descriptions	
8. Delegation	
9. Quality	
10. Performance appraisals	
11. Team spirit	
12. Commitment	
Total	

*Maximum total possible is 108; minimum total possible is 12.

Chapter Six

One Step at a Time

Using Teamwork To Meet Strategic Plans

T om Bailey is a vice president for State Bank and Trust, a branch of a large bank holding company. He has been in this position for two years and reports to Henry Moorehead, the bank president. He has been requested to spend some time with the new human resources director who is conducting a series of interviews as part of his orientation to the bank.

Tom leaned forward and rested his left forearm on the table. He stared idly out the window before finally turning to Ed Jones, the human resources director.

TOM: You want me to tell you what this team is like? Well, that may take some time, but I've got it if you have.

Ed nodded agreeably. Since coming to State Bank and Trust only a few weeks ago he had sought out occasions for talks just like this. He sensed that the thing he most needed in this new post was a feel for the real issues.

TOM: Well, for openers, I guess we really are not a team. We don't work together that much. You know, I hadn't thought about that in a long time. It bothered me at first. When I was in corporate trust, they really had us honed into shape.

ED: You're from corporate?

TOM: Yeah, they needed someone to add a few touches here and I guess I drew short straw. At first, I made a lot of noise about meetings, but I soon learned that neither the boss nor the guys were really interested. The few meetings we held were actually funny. We even voted on the interest spread we would target for next year. It was like that all the time. We couldn't really come to grips with differences. I remember Charlie and Bob had a big set-to and the boss reassigned the project.

ED: Then, I guess, Henry is calling the tune?

TOM: No, I don't see it that way. I suppose you can say as boss he has final responsibility — but this is really a team condition. We just don't like conflict and when it happens we negotiate one-to-one. You should see the politicking when it's a big decision.

ED: Big decision?

TOM: Yeah, like the budget cuts last year. Cover yourself all the way. In the end we wound up taking cuts across the board. That meant we all shared the misery. It wasn't right — especially when the new line could have used more resources behind it. I'm as guilty as the next guy. I held out for my two bits. Say, why am I telling you all this anyway?

ED: Guess I've got a kindly face. But it's a good question. Why don't you open up in the team?

TOM: It wouldn't be popular. Popularity is in, you know. Our whole communication pattern is superficial. Everybody edits his stuff — no one wants to stand out.

ED: You mean you've got a bunch of party types keeping the place happy?

TOM: No, not that. We talk business. A lot. But it's all filtered — lukewarm. Even when there's something really bad, we cook up some good to lay in with it.

ED: I don't understand.

TOM: Well, take last year when the Internal Revenue Service reports went out late. Somebody should have been laid out in spades. Well, there wasn't any real facing up. No one wanted to put the finger on anyone else, so we wrote it into the monthly report sandwiched between a couple of modest claims to fame. I'll bet the chairman didn't miss it. I felt a little guilty about covering up the mistake and we didn't learn a damned thing—we still don't know how it happened.

ED: But surely the boss . . .

TOM: No, it's us. He tries to make the great leap forward once in a while. When we put the annual plan together, he saw possibilities of a real breakout. He wanted to cut bait on the losing lines, but the team held back. In the end, rather than cutting the losing line he wound up negotiating with every one of us for a few added percents to meet the desired objectives. It's a case of us being committed to a little progress a step at a time.

ED: Do you know that?

TOM: You know, I guess that's another thing that gets under my skin. I don't really know where the negotiation ends with everyone. I'm always a little suspicious that I got the short end of the budget.

ED: Why don't you go to Henry and confront the issue?

TOM: It might help, but then he would worry about facing the others—especially if we did it all together in a meeting. That is, if we ever had such a meeting. No, keep a good, steady pace, keep your nose clean. Do your own job and make each year just a mite better. That's the norm and, by damn, do we live by the rules!

ED: Rules?

TOM: Yeah! We've got regulation on regulation. Every time we get an unusual problem, we legislate a safe way around it. We use regulations to keep everything "fair and firm." See that stuff on my desk? We've even got a damn rule for water jugs.

ED: And you negotiate your plans and policies?

TOM: Sure, we keep that all loose. Some overall direction, but the detail isn't so tight you can't maneuver.

ED: You sure sound unhappy.

TOM: I am.

ED: And it's not Henry's fault?

TOM: I don't think so. It's mine — and George's and Charlie's and Bob's — all of us. We're just locked up. When Henry came here two years ago, we all felt he asked a bunch of good questions and he had some good suggestions. But he spent the first year depending on us. We knew all the problems. We knew the files and the rules. He wanted to break out — had some good ideas. He just got cautious about squaring off with us. He still needs every one of us. He'd be helpless.

So, Ed, how are you going to help us?

Open disagreement and conflict are avoided on this team even when such discussion could lead to breakthroughs in higher quality results. So that they do not have to face up to the important and difficult issues facing them, team members edit their comments to sound as positive as possible. Henry, the boss, is perhaps the most influential avoider of conflict on the team — he "settles" a disagreement between two people by reassigning the project.

Working at a "good steady pace" is accepted as good enough for this team. If they were to challenge themselves to the highest performance possible, it would run counter to the way they are comfortably operating. Henry's good ideas about new directions were quickly subdued by members used to their habits of preserving the status quo.

Always sticking to the rules gives this team the security that comes from a predictable way of handling problems. Members feel comfortable knowing that any conflict will be cushioned by sticking to the rules or by soft peddling negative comments.

The team kept all of their goals and objectives within comfortable reach and then Henry negotiated with each member individually. This, no doubt, held them back from a full teamwide determination of strategically important goals.

In such an atmosphere, where popularity is more important than accurate feedback and critique, little or no learning from experience is possible, and excellence is nearly unattainable.

Teamwork Dimensions

In the 5,5 exercise of power and authority leadership is based on accepting the status quo, seeking to make some progress, and trying to avoid losing ground. Disagreements, if they do arise, are adjusted by dealing with people individually in order that compromise and accommodation may be achieved without direct confrontation. Procedures, systems, rules, and regulations are employed not so much to organize and use information but to control people, keep them in step, and mechanically arbitrate differences that arise.

Goals and objectives of a 5,5 culture are likely to be short-term targets that are formulated as extensions of the past and aimed at maximizing the present situation.

Norms and standards are likely to stress doing better than last year or being above average in performance. Progress is rated in terms of inadequate past criteria—not in terms of excellent present criteria.

Job assignments are based on a mechanical division of responsibilities so that no one is asked to bear an unfair share of the burden. Adherence to job descriptions and standard procedures maintains coordination without calling on members to exercise personal judgments.

Critique and feedback tend to be superficial. When feedback is negative, it is often sandwiched between positive affirmation of performance. Morale and cohesion in the 5,5 culture may be based on an "in" feeling. Status, that is, who and not what you know, and politics are what count. Being dependable, even-tempered, and willing to compromise are part of the "team spirit."

Diagnosis of Teamwork

The following statements and scales will assist you in determining the extent to which your own team contains elements of the 5,5 culture. Rate the statements from 1 (uncharacteristic) to 9 (highly characteristic) as a description of your team.

1. Directions: Adequate guidelines are provided for accomplishing tasks; directions are tempered by consideration of individual resistances.

1	2	3	4	5	6	7	8	9
Completely uncharacteristic				Partially characteristic				Highly characteristic

2. Meetings: Usually an extension of previous topics, discussions convey the implicit assumption that majority thinking is to prevail.

1	2	3	4	5	6	7	8	9

Completely uncharacteristic   Partially characteristic   Highly characteristic

3. Conflict: Members sense when they have pushed their positions far enough and back off as necessary to meet others halfway.

1	2	3	4	5	6	7	8	9

Completely uncharacteristic   Partially characteristic   Highly characteristic

4. Objectives: Objectives are scaled to what members are prepared to accept.

1	2	3	4	5	6	7	8	9

Completely uncharacteristic   Partially characteristic   Highly characteristic

5. Innovation: New ideas which find acceptance are basically modifications of present ways of doing things.

1	2	3	4	5	6	7	8	9

Completely uncharacteristic   Partially characteristic   Highly characteristic

6. Communication (candor): Information is filtered or edited so that what is said is consistent with organizational demands and other members' expectations.

1	2	3	4	5	6	7	8	9

Completely uncharacteristic   Partially characteristic   Highly characteristic

7. Job descriptions: Work assignments have evolved and are based more on tradition, precedent, and personality than on the nature of the tasks to be performed.

1	2	3	4	5	6	7	8	9

Completely uncharacteristic   Partially characteristic   Highly characteristic

8. Delegation: Assignment of projects is mechanical with each member given a "fair share" of the task within limits of ability, time, or commitment.

1	2	3	4	5	6	7	8	9

Completely uncharacteristic   Partially characteristic   Highly characteristic

9. Quality: Attitudes toward quality are that existing standards, even though allowing for deviations, are sufficient.

1	2	3	4	5	6	7	8	9

Completely uncharacteristic   Partially characteristic   Highly characteristic

10. Performance appraisals: Criticisms are sandwiched in between praises and compliments.

1	2	3	4	5	6	7	8	9
Completely uncharacteristic				Partially characteristic			Highly characteristic	

11. Team spirit: There is a spirit of hail-fellow-well-met, reinforced by "going along to get along."

1	2	3	4	5	6	7	8	9
Completely uncharacteristic				Partially characteristic			Highly characteristic	

12. Commitment: Commitment arises from the prestige of being a member in good standing of a "good organization."

1	2	3	4	5	6	7	8	9
Completely uncharacteristic				Partially characteristic			Highly characteristic	

In the following chart total your ratings for each scale.*
Transfer your total to the 5,5 column in Figure 9.1. An interpretation of the numbers is provided in Chapter 9.

Scale	Rating
1. Directions	
2. Meetings	
3. Conflict	
4. Objectives	
5. Innovation	
6. Communication	
7. Job descriptions	
8. Delegation	
9. Quality	
10. Performance appraisals	
11. Team spirit	
12. Commitment	
Total	

*Maximum total possible is 108; minimum total possible is 12.

Chapter Seven

When the End Justifies the Means

Developing a Shared Purpose

C arol Birnie is the head of data processing for a large domestic airline. She reports directly to Joe Tagliani, the president. She has concluded that the data processing division has need of a powerful and expensive computer to expand her operations. To support her position, she has tried to enlist the support of the company's auditor.

"Carol, you'll never get away with it."

It was the voice of Gene Harley, newest addition to the masthead of a distinguished auditing firm. Carol was looking out of the window of her office; she turned away and faced Gene.

CAROL: Not only am I going to get away with it, I'm going to get a solid round of appreciation for my wisdom and foresight. And you're going to help me do it!

GENE: Carol, I don't think I can support your proposal. It's just far too much hardware for a company of this size. You could run General Motors with a mainframe like that. Besides I don't see how auditors should be involved in the evaluation of a capital proposal.

CAROL: Gene, you owe me one. Remember year-end closing when you were desperate? You had 12 companies after you and two of your guys off sick. I put four people and a lot of hardware at your disposal. They combed out all the time-draining trivia, gave you summaries, samples, audit trails—the whole schmear. Cut your time here in half—and, I might add, without a change in audit fee. It's your turn to scratch my back.

Gene reddened. He recalled the desperation of the year-end. A knock on the door interrupted his embarrassment as Sue Radcliff, the chief programmer, entered.

There was room for more embarrassment as Carol took the printout, scanned it briefly, and proceeded to chew out Sue in front of him. Sue mumbled something about doing better next time as she retreated.

GENE: Carol, it's not my business, but you shouldn't have done that. Sue's a bright girl. And her data were right on. She just couldn't push that proposal you're aiming for.

CAROL: Gene, you're right. It is none of your business. What is your business is an auditor support. Do I get it or do you want a little extra work next quarter-end?

GENE: That's blackmail.

CAROL: Such an ugly word. Let's call it creative accounting.

GENE: Look, I hear you. But Tagliani's no fool. Those growth assumptions will stand out. If my senior partners got wind of this, they'd roast my brain for breakfast. This airline is in a growth industry, but the scale of what you're proposing is an order of magnitude beyond your needs.

CAROL: Gene, let me handle Tagliani. He's an old-timer. Tough, yes, but he's not up on computers. He passed the half-life of an executive about 10 years ago. He doesn't know a bit from a byte. I can skate around him easily. All it takes is a little technical jargon, a word or two of appreciation of his wisdom and foresight, and admiration for his sterling leadership—and a little creative accounting.

GENE: He'll see through it. It's megabucks and it'll strain cash flow.

CAROL: We'll lease, Gene. And I want a clear statement of support from a distinguished audit company. Joe Tagliani's an old fool. He's dependent on you and me in these areas.

He's still dreaming about flying our first Lockheed Constellation.

GENE: All right. I'll look it over. I don't want to fight a war with the client. It still looks too grand to me. Your financial people will be a tough hurdle.

CAROL: Gene, I mean to take over financial. Every day that goes by, I get a little stronger and they get a little weaker.

Just then the telephone rang. Carol picked it up. It was Frank McDonald. Sweetness came into her words.

CAROL: Top of the morning to you, Frank. Yes, I wanted to talk to you. Got a minute now? Fine, I'll be right over.

Turning to Gene, she said, "Remember year-end, Gene."
"Poor old Frank," thought Gene. He shook his head slowly, and said aloud, "Carol, can I level with you?"

CAROL: Yes, of course.

GENE: I'm worried about the direction of data processing. As an auditor I am supposed to ensure the quality and accuracy of financial matters, but I can't help having a feeling of concern for the company's general good health.

I look at you and your department and I can't help but feel the interests of the company are secondary to your own careers and personal ambitions, and to sophistication for its own sake, not for its practical value.

CAROL: I don't see how you can say that. I have some very high standards.

GENE: Yes, but your standards of growth, sophistication, technical superiority, and the latest fads are not what the company really needs. Your people are serving you and not the company.

CAROL: That's a damned lie.

GENE: I don't think so. You support your people, true. You deal with them ever so nicely, but always one to one. Closed doors. No team meetings. No open reviews. And each project leader is a tight little island. One-upmanship and back-stabbing, everyone competing for his own turf with more or less a blank check from you — a company check. The cost is staggering.

CAROL: That's not fair. You have no right to say that.

GENE: Yes, I do. I'm concerned. Concerned for Tagliani and the company.

CAROL: You attended our quarterly progress review. Wasn't that impressive?

GENE: It sure was. The same people that were backstabbing in private were now giving wide-eyed praise. It's nice to have no risk of being undercut. Yours is a very competitive department and most of your people are taking advantage of a big budget to do all the things they always wanted to do.

CAROL: I think you've said quite enough. I run a top-notch department, and we have a mandate to put this company on the leading edge. We're doing that. How I decide to manage my people is my damn business. Now, I want that support for the new mainframe. Do I get it, or do you want to invest in some midnight oil? It's as simple as that, Mr. Auditor. Think it over.

The door closed and she was gone.

The clearly opportunistic behavior of Carol and those on her team is highlighted by the auditor's observation that the interests of the company appear to be secondary to personal goals.

In order to further her own position, Carol behaves differently, depending on the status of the people with whom she is dealing. When she is dealing with superiors such as Tagliani, she gushes admiration, respect, and "sweetness." When she is trying to gain support from her peer, Gene Harley, she negotiates and reminds him that he owes her a favor. When she is speaking to subordinates such as Sue Radcliff, she tries to exploit them as fully as possible for her own purposes.

Across Carol's whole team there is an atmosphere of one-upmanship and backstabbing. Rather than adhering to standards that represent consistently high quality contributions to the company, this team pursues technical sophistication as a way of expanding their power base. There is little or no regard for whether the expansions make strategic sense.

There is likely to be very little sense of shared purpose or group loyalty in a team in which each member is on his or her own course. This lack of shared purpose is compounded by the members' isolation from one another and by Carol's management style of directing each person's work individually with little teamwide discussion or coordination. Individual job assignments are made on a one-to-one, closed door basis. Therefore, the team is unable to review their actions effectively or to plan for changes which will strategically direct the team toward excellence. Another reason there is no candid critique on this team is that the members are busy trying to gain favors and manipulate the facts. They do this by covering their private backstabbing with public praise.

Carol and her team members do not tie their own achievement with the achievement of company objectives. Rather, they see the building of a personal power base as a separate and higher priority, an end which drives their whole manner of operating in the team. Excellence becomes secondary to personal gain.

Teamwork Dimensions

In the opportunistic team culture, power and authority are seen as instruments to attain personal ends. Thus the boss and team members exercise power where they have it (i.e., subordinates), seek to gain leverage by obligating colleagues, and cast themselves in a favorable light by deference to those at higher levels. The team's goals and objectives are merely extensions of the personal goals of its members. As such, the team objectives are frequently to gain control and power in relation to other teams rather than to further organizational productivity.

Norms and standards with respect to performance may be high as the team seeks to further its position within the company. However, these norms and standards arc bcst characterized as devious and unprincipled.

Job assignments are determined by the boss with a view to whose work can most effectively enhance his or her reputation. Subordinates vie with one another for assignments most likely to be seen as important to the boss, and they frequently undercut one another in the process.

In an opportunistic team culture, critique and feedback are likely to take the form of praise and compliments in public and considerable criticism and backbiting in private. A key assumption in this culture is that advancing one's own interests is frequently achieved by invidious comparison. Thus in the opportunistic culture, feedback and critique are not seen or used for constructive purposes. Morale and cohesion in this culture are likely to be akin to a roller coaster ride with wild swings of ups and downs depending on the success or failure of the moment.

Diagnosis of Teamwork

The following statements and scales will assist you in determining the extent to which your own team contains elements of the opportunistic culture. Rate the statements from 1 (uncharacteristic) to 9 (highly characteristic) as a description of your team.

1. Directions: To be seen in the best possible light, directions from above are accepted without question but subordinates are provided detailed instructions to carry out orders with no deviations permitted.

1	2	3	4	5	6	7	8	9
Completely uncharacteristic				Partially characteristic				Highly characteristic

2. Meetings: Members have hidden agendas designed to promote self-advancement; one-to-one meetings are common even when issues discussed have teamwide significance.

1	2	3	4	5	6	7	8	9
Completely uncharacteristic				Partially characteristic				Highly characteristic

3. Conflict: Conflict is hidden or disguised as members maneuver to gain their objectives.

1	2	3	4	5	6	7	8	9

Completely   Partially   Highly
uncharacteristic   characteristic   characteristic

4. Objectives: Objectives are couched in whatever terms thought wanted by upper levels.

1	2	3	4	5	6	7	8	9

Completely   Partially   Highly
uncharacteristic   characteristic   characteristic

5. Innovation: New ideas are not welcomed unless they can be used to elevate the status of the leader.

1	2	3	4	5	6	7	8	9

Completely   Partially   Highly
uncharacteristic   characteristic   characteristic

6. Communication (candor): Ideas and opinions are expressed in a guarded fashion to avoid seeming out of step and to avoid exposure of weakness.

1	2	3	4	5	6	7	8	9

Completely   Partially   Highly
uncharacteristic   characteristic   characteristic

7. Job descriptions: Team members are defensive of their positions and seek to expand their spheres of influence.

1	2	3	4	5	6	7	8	9

Completely   Partially   Highly
uncharacteristic   characteristic   characteristic

8. Delegation: Team members vie with one another for choice assignments and "plums."

1	2	3	4	5	6	7	8	9

Completely   Partially   Highly
uncharacteristic   characteristic   characteristic

9. Quality: Quality is saluted as a means of gaining recognition; actions do not reflect genuine concern for quality.

1	2	3	4	5	6	7	8	9

Completely   Partially   Highly
uncharacteristic   characteristic   characteristic

10. Performance appraisals: Performance reviews focus on shortcomings which reflect adversely on the team; to encourage greater effort members are pitted against one another.

1	2	3	4	5	6	7	8	9

Completely   Partially   Highly
uncharacteristic   characteristic   characteristic

11. Team spirit: Favors are given with the implicit understanding they will be repaid at an opportune time; sly ways of undercutting others to enhance one's own position are not uncommon.

1	2	3	4	5	6	7	8	9

Completely   Partially   Highly
uncharacteristic   characteristic   characteristic

12. Commitment: Members are motivated to advance their personal interests rather than to contribute to team or organizational goals.

1	2	3	4	5	6	7	8	9
Completely uncharacteristic				Partially characteristic				Highly characteristic

In the following chart total your ratings for each scale.*
Transfer your total to the Opportunism column in Figure 9.1.
An interpretation of the numbers is provided in Chapter 9.

Scale	Rating
1. Directions	
2. Meetings	
3. Conflict	
4. Objectives	
5. Innovation	
6. Communication	
7. Job descriptions	
8. Delegation	
9. Quality	
10. Performance appraisals	
11. Team spirit	
12. Commitment	
Total	

*Maximum total possible is 108; minimum total possible is 12.

Chapter Eight

When $1 + 1 = 3$

How a High Performing Team Does It

F lat Creek is an older manufacturing facility that produces a variety of metallic goods used in the production of consumer products. It had been in a steady decline for several years before Peter Burnside, the plant manager, had taken over. At about the same time Peter arrived a number of senior managers retired, and Peter had assembled a new management team from other locations in the corporation. Since that time the plant performance has improved to the point at which it is now the highest production facility in the corporation.

"Whap."

The squash ball hit low and close to the corner, returning with drive force to right court. Joe Segal made a desperate lunge. The sound of his fall echoed in a combination of soft thuds and the wooden clatter of his racquet.

PETER: Game and match!

JOE: Dammit, Peter, I don't know how you do it (muttered Joe as he painfully drew himself back to his feet). Three matches and you haven't even broken sweat.

Peter Burnside grinned, wiped his forehead on the towel, and said:

PETER: See — sweat. You'll take me in another three months. After all, you've just begun. It's a lot different than tennis. It takes a while to get used to the angles.

The door clanked open and the two stepped out. A few minutes later they stood in the showers. A layer of steam formed on the ceiling.

JOE: Carter sent me down from headquarters. Wants to know how you do it.

PETER: Do what?

JOE: You know what I mean. Carter watches the production reports. You've got the oldest plant in the company, yet you've shot up to the top of the stats. He wants to know — in detail — what you do to make that pile of junk perform.

PETER: Oh no, not again. I told you last time. It's broken in and I've got some good people.

JOE: Come on, Peter. It was broken in 30 years ago and I know you took the ragtags of the operation when you came down here. You asked to give John Huckle a chance after Bill Montgomery wanted to fire him. And Jim Hughes hadn't done anything for a couple of years. Not since the plant start-up. Then there's Bud Fisher from the head office — a real pain-in-the-neck — pushing for a transfer to Bob Johnson's outfit before he came here. You even took Susan Bradley, who was going to quit before you came along. Carter calls your team "the dirty half dozen."

PETER: Joe, I'm a little sensitive about my people. They weren't ragtags. They're good people. They just got caught in circumstances that limited them. Judgments like that don't sit easy with me. You talked with them before. You're a human resources man. You know the talent that's there. Here at Flat Creek, they pitched right in.

JOE: Sorry, Peter. I should know better. They came together here and you sparked them into life.

PETER: I wish you'd stop making me into a miracle worker. I recognized their talent and brought them together. I've said it before and I'll say it again. It was a real team effort. We made it together.

After a short breakfast at Joe's hotel, Peter drove them to the plant where they made a quick tour of some new buildings before the morning shift began operation.

Later, they sat in Peter's office, each with a mug of black coffee. Peter glanced through the previous night's production reports and called Bud Fisher. It was 8:28 A.M.

PETER: Bud, did you get to see the off spec on number 2 press? I think we may have a bad die. (There was a pause, punctuated by the occasional "Uh huh.") Hey, that sounds just fine. You guys sure got a network. What time did they call you? I'll take MOC the rest of the week if you like. Naw, no problem. I know you're expecting company.

JOE: What's MOC?

PETER: Manager on call. Mostly it doesn't amount to anything. The supervisors handle things very well and the union stewards kick in if the supervisor isn't available. Still, this is a very old facility and we try to anticipate major problems like, say, a water main break, or a flash flood in the creek. I don't expect to be called, and it's no special burden to stay available.

JOE: But why you? Aren't you the guy who said you don't buy a dog and do your own barking?

Peter grinned sheepishly.

PETER: That's not one of my best quotes, but we really do believe in delegation. My serving as MOC is helpful to the others and it keeps me in touch with day-to-day things. Ordinarily, though, people are given the opportunity to handle as much as they are capable of without having to clear things with a senior manager or me. The new fad is to call it empowerment, but it's the same thing. (A bell sounded briefly from the plant floor.) Eight-thirty. First break. The mechanics relieve the press operators for 10 or 15 minutes. Press operation is pretty repetitious and we like to provide regular breaks to avoid self-hypnosis or something like that. Besides, the mechanics get to know the real pattern of the press and understand the operator's log notes. All the guys can read a press by the rhythm of the sound. A millisecond out and they can tell what's up.

JOE: You wouldn't get away with that in Gardenvale. The trades people are really uptight.

PETER: We couldn't do it here a year or so ago. John talked it over with the hourly employees when we were in prenegotiation.

JOE: Prenegotiation? What's that?

PETER: Well, before we exchange contract proposals, we sit down with the union and talk about problems and differences and we develop answers for each other. It saves a lot of time and keeps the contract thin.

JOE: Who thought of that?

PETER: I don't know. We work together. It's really hard to pinpoint who did what.

JOE: You're going to keep dodging the issue, aren't you? Carter wants to know what you are doing.

PETER: Joe, if I could tell you, I would. We just don't stand on a lot of ceremony. We *all* run the plant.

JOE: But give it to me a step at a time. You started with almost a whole new set of managers in a plant that was at the bottom of the heap.

PETER: I got interested in teamwork as a management process a long time ago. I went to a seminar that had a real theory base. It put me in touch with myself and what I am inclined to do as a team member or team leader that can make a difference. That experience gave me insights into the dynamics of teamwork as well as into myself. Flat Creek offered me the chance to try these things out, to see if they would work.

The first thing I did was to review this approach with the group to see if they were interested in doing an experiment to put that stuff to work. Coming to Flat Creek, we had no place to go but up.

The second step was for them to get a firsthand experience in the concepts and in getting feedback on their effectiveness. I got a lot of Missouri-type, "show me," feedback in the beginning but they came around. You could see and feel the changes that were taking place. You could see mutual respect grow. It was a great experience.

In the third step we turned the plant over to our subordinates and spent several concentrated days on team building. We studied ourselves and how we had been working together to see how we could get even more synergy than we had begun to experience. It's like that now.

This place is like a research and development lab in human effectiveness. We research what we're doing while we do it, pool our resources, make decisions, and keep our eye on the implementation to see how well it's working. The good news is that this approach is permeating right down to the bottom—and into the union.

It's interesting that you brought up the stats, but that's almost looking in the rearview mirror. What we're really proud of is the decision made upstairs to give us a major capital expansion. This shows us that Carter and his people think we're a safe place to invest.

There were a lot of other things in the beginning. Sitting down with all the players, I guess you'd call it—the customers, the union, the hourly workers, the clerical and accounting staff, old guard and my—what did you call it?—dirty half dozen.

JOE: What came first?

PETER: The idea of working the problems as a team effort. We divided the responsibility for gathering information about problems. I'd planned to do it, but Bud suggested we should handle it in pairs—discuss the outcome; devil's advocate and all.

JOE: Sounds sensible.

PETER: It was. I remember our first meeting with the data we had gathered. It's a wonder we had a business left. The customers and the union were really angry. Well, we spent half a day and set up the plant operation the way we wanted it to be. Susan put that one in. She thought that if we had an objective we could operate toward it, rather than cut and patch the past. It was really brilliant.

JOE: But simple.

PETER: The best ideas are simple.

JOE: Go on.

PETER: It's all sort of foggy. One move blends with another, but over the next few weeks, we looked at how the jobs were set up, what kind of meetings were needed, and what personal hang-ups we had. It was exciting. We ended with a couple of new team objectives—improving quality with the goal of zero defects and getting the union on board. We gave ourselves 90 days for that and did it in half the time.

JOE: Sounds like a lot of meetings.

PETER: Not really. We divided it up into individual work, pairs, and trios. I kind of sat back then and orchestrated. A symphony conductor shouldn't have an overwhelming desire to blow on the bassoon.

JOE: Lazy devil.

PETER: Yeah, but I put in a lot of hours. I was kept advised of everything, but we never made a team decision. It was always an individual named to be responsible — sometimes me, if it was a big deal, mostly others.

JOE: Weren't you afraid of losing control?

PETER: Joe, revolutionary though it may be, I feel that the best way to use power is to share it. I keep advised, but the guys know their responsibilities and they don't bring me trivia. Once in a while we talk about how things are going.

JOE: I suppose you're going to lay that off on someone else too?

PETER: Yup. Jim started it off as a model project, small "e" experiment.

JOE: Peter, I've got a confession. Gardenvale's a mess. Can you handle it too?

PETER: I like it here and I like this team. We can handle anything here. I do need a bit to chew on, though, and I'd like to try this kind of experiment all over again . . . . Why not collapse Gardenvale into here? We could use new presses. And the way that whole area is booming we shouldn't have any trouble selling off the property. Acme or some of those other companies would love to have any of our surplus people.

JOE: Carter won't go for it.

PETER: Why?

JOE: It wasn't his idea.

PETER: Let me try it on him. It would reduce overhead by something close to half. It would stretch us to the limit. I can think of all kinds of economies of scale.

JOE: Boy, that takes it! I came down here to get you hooked for a new job and you wind up reorganizing the company.

PETER: It was Jim Hughes' idea. Honest. We've already been thinking about it.

All of the members of Peter's team challenge themselves and one another to the fullest degree possible through active initiative and inquiry. When there is a problem to be solved, the person closest to it reports it, investigates it, or initiates actions to be taken. Each team member makes appropriate contributions as he or she and others deem such a contribution to be strategically useful — even when the issue at hand isn't a part of that person's job description.

Peter set the stage for such a high-quality approach as soon as he came on board as boss. He assumed responsibility for sitting down with all the players and coming to a clear understanding of what was needed to bring about a drastic turnaround in productivity.

Peter consistently gives his team credit for assuming responsibilities that move the team toward high-level accomplishment. The manager-on-call duty is a good example of coordinated action toward a common goal. Peter's team spent considerable effort setting and clarifying their goals with a high priority given to the understanding of these goals by all team members and the setting of a clear time frame within which to meet them. As a result the team achieved their top-priority goals in half the time allotted.

The "dirty half dozen" clearly enjoy the challenges facing them; Peter describes their work as exciting. All of the individuals—who had low morale in their previous work settings—wholeheartedly joined in when the new Flat Creek culture began to emerge.

Open feedback and critique have been brought into use as a standard part of the team's modus operandi. Regular communications about plant issues allow them to discuss potential problems before hidden resentments and locked-in attitudes develop. Personal feedback of the kind Peter provided to Joe (about Peter's response to Joe's disparaging comments about other team members) is honest and constructive.

Peter's team is ready to meet any challenge because members have a clear understanding of the tasks at hand and a deep commitment to achieving them in the best way possible. Their proactive mode is demonstrated when they had anticipated the next logical steps for dealing with the Gardenvale problem. For them this means that members understand and take on responsibility for the work interdependently, rather than independently. Synergy is regularly achieved.

Teamwork Dimensions

In the 9,9 exercise of power and authority the boss stimulates others to become involved in problems and committed to solutions through shared participation. Each team member has a voice in the outcome and thus feels responsible for a positive contribution to both team tasks and individual activities.

Goals and objectives oriented in a 9,9 way are based on standards of excellence and are geared to increasing the involvement of those responsible for achieving them. In this way the integration of individual and organizational goals is achieved, and people willingly give their personal commitment to bringing about their success.

Norms and standards, which are based on mutual understanding and commitment among team members, are established by determining conditions that will permit excellent performance. Such standards do not happen by accident; they are created by intent and become operational by conscious effort. Team members continually hold one another accountable for performance that meets these standards.

Individual competencies for solving problems is the primary criterion for determining who does what. Even though greater demands may be placed on one team member than another, teamwork goals are achieved in the most effective manner. Work assignments are also used to provide less competent members with opportunities for developing skills which advance team objectives. Substitutional interdependence among members is relied on to maintain continuity of effort.

Open and candid feedback and critique are used extensively to examine team performance and to learn from it. Members are able to examine problems from the perspective of "what is right" rather than "who is right" and "how can we do better" rather than "who or what is to blame." Morale and cohesion are characterized by positive feelings and emotions and a readiness to be involved and committed. There is a high degree of trust among team members who find many ways to support one another.

Diagnosis of Teamwork

The following statements and scales will assist you in determining the extent to which your own team contains elements of the 9,9 culture. Rate the statements from 1 (uncharacteristic) to 9 (highly characteristic) as a description of your team.

1. Directions: Clear instructions for carrying out responsibilities are provided with opportunity available to clarify unclear areas; everyone understands what is to be done and why it is important.

1	2	3	4	5	6	7	8	9

Completely	Partially	Highly
uncharacteristic	characteristic	characteristic

2. Meetings: Action steps are reached by utilizing the resources of everyone who has something to contribute.

1	2	3	4	5	6	7	8	9

Completely	Partially	Highly
uncharacteristic	characteristic	characteristic

3. Conflict: Points of disagreement are made explicit and reasons for them are identified to resolve underlying causes.

1	2	3	4	5	6	7	8	9

Completely	Partially	Highly
uncharacteristic	characteristic	characteristic

4. Objectives: Members are involved in setting, reviewing, and evaluating those objectives on which their performance can have an impact.

1	2	3	4	5	6	7	8	9

Completely	Partially	Highly
uncharacteristic	characteristic	characteristic

5. Innovation: Creativity and innovation are stimulated by the readiness to experiment.

1	2	3	4	5	6	7	8	9

Completely uncharacteristic Partially characteristic Highly characteristic

6. Communication (candor): Members are well-informed and participate in problem analysis and decision making; differences are openly discussed and worked through for sound understanding.

1	2	3	4	5	6	7	8	9

Completely uncharacteristic Partially characteristic Highly characteristic

7. Job descriptions: Responsibilities are designed around the nature of tasks and qualifications of members in ways that maximize interaction between those who share the action.

1	2	3	4	5	6	7	8	9

Completely uncharacteristic Partially characteristic Highly characteristic

8. Delegation: Degree of autonomy in completing assignments is matched to individual capacity for exercising responsible interdependence.

1	2	3	4	5	6	7	8	9

Completely uncharacteristic Partially characteristic Highly characteristic

9. Quality: High quality standards receive full commitment from team members; outstanding performance is achieved and maintained because members are motivated to excel.

1	2	3	4	5	6	7	8	9

Completely uncharacteristic   Partially characteristic   Highly characteristic

10. Performance appraisals: Performance appraisals are based on previously jointly agreed criteria with realistic review of strengths and weaknesses on a two-way feedback basis.

1	2	3	4	5	6	7	8	9

Completely uncharacteristic   Partially characteristic   Highly characteristic

11. Team spirit: Cohesion and team loyalty lead to mutual assistance when it is needed.

1	2	3	4	5	6	7	8	9

Completely uncharacteristic   Partially characteristic   Highly characteristic

12. Commitment: Commitment comes from members having a common stake in teamwide success; personal gratification is from making needed contributions.

1	2	3	4	5	6	7	8	9

Completely uncharacteristic   Partially characteristic   Highly characteristic

In the following chart total your ratings for each scale.* Transfer your total to the 9,9 column in Figure 9.1. An interpretation of the numbers is provided in Chapter 9.

Scale	Rating
1. Directions	
2. Meetings	
3. Conflict	
4. Objectives	
5. Innovation	
6. Communication	
7. Job descriptions	
8. Delegation	
9. Quality	
10. Performance appraisals	
11. Team spirit	
12. Commitment	
Total	

*Maximum total possible is 108; minimum total possible is 12.

Chapter Nine

Diagnosing Your Team's Actual Grid Culture

T he vignettes in Chapters 2 through 8 provide a diagnostic mirror through which you may have seen the characteristics of your own team and its culture. A comparison of the evaluation scales at the end of those chapters gives you a clearer picture of your team.

Place the ratings from Chapters 2 through 8 in the Total Ratings boxes on the last row of the Team Culture Summary Sheet in Figure 9.1. (The ratings from Chapter 2 should be placed in the 9,1 column; the ratings from Chapter 3 go in the 1,9 column, Chapter 4 in the third column, labeled paternal-

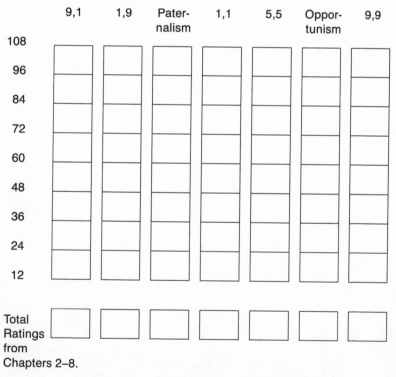

9,1	1,9	Pater-nalism	1,1	5,5	Oppor-tunism	9,9

108
96
84
72
60
48
36
24
12

Total Ratings from Chapters 2–8.

Figure 9.1. Team culture summary sheet.

ism, and so on. Chapter 5 is 1,1; 6, 5,5; 7, opportunism; and 8 is 9,9.) The graph below shows the Teamwork Grid® styles in the same sequence as they appear in the chapters. Next, plot the scores on the bar graph in the same sequence as shown in Figure 9.2.

Generally speaking, your highest score represents what you think to be your team's dominant Teamwork Grid® style. The next highest score is your team's backup Teamwork Grid® style, and so on until your lowest score. The lowest score represents the most rejected Teamwork Grid® style for characterizing your team. If the scores of three or more Teamwork Grid® styles are close, it might mean that team members are responding to one another in a stimulus-response way; or team members are acting independently of one another, almost without teamness; or that the team culture is inconsistent.

As a set of benchmark numbers you might consider the following. The maximum "score" that you could assign to any team Grid® style is 108 and the minimum score is 12. Any score of, say, 84 to 108 reflects the presence in your team of a high amount of that Grid style; score of 60 to 83 represents the presence of some of that Grid style; 37 to 59 means there is not much of this style in your team; whereas 12 to 36 indicates an almost complete absence of the Teamwork Grid® style in your team.

Figure 9.2 shows how to do it.

Look at the summary for Team 1. These data represent scales completed by Peter Burnside's team from Chapter 8. It is evident that this team is characterized as operating to a significant degree in the 9,9 style, earning 84 points out of a total of 108. The next most prevalent style is paternalism with 42 points, indicating this as the backup style for Peter's team. The other styles are not present to any significant degree.

Spectacular Teamwork

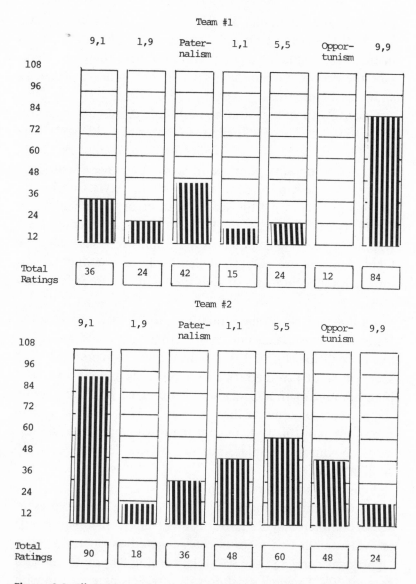

Figure 9.2. Illustrations of team culture summary sheet for two different teams.

Peter described their team building activities in Chapter 8, and it appears his team has derived much benefit from them.

Now let's examine the data for Team 2 which represent scales taken from Cindy and Sam's team in Chapter 2. The story of Team 2 is told in the 9,1 column where 90 points are assigned. That means the team is operating in a strong 9,1 way, and a dominant Teamwork Grid® style with that strength is certainly something to think about. The 60 points in the 5,5 column indicate a relatively strong backup style. The episode described in Chapter 2 shows a team where fighting to achieve individual objectives is the norm and where fights are frequently settled by compromise born of exasperation. This seems to substantiate the data that shows a strong 9,1 dominant style and a significant 5,5 backup. The other styles are less prevalent and are overshadowed by the strong dominant and backup style.

Could Team 2 benefit from team building? The Team 1 profile tells us, at least if the data can be accepted at face value, that that team is moving in a right direction. It has an open, confronting, conflict-solving, problem-solving character to it, and team building obviously contributed to their effectiveness. Team 2, which is characterized as having a dominant team style of 9,1 with a 5,5 backup, also stands to gain much by doing team building in a sound and successful manner. This team may find that it has a long way to go in order to mobilize the resources available to the fullest. It may come to recognize that participation is uneven and that there is a much greater need for widespread two-way participation than currently is characteristic of it.

Having taken this step, you may wish to take another before proceeding further. The next step might be for you to involve the other members of your team in reading this book, asking each to complete the scales just as you have done, and suggesting that when everyone has completed the assignment, the data can be summarized so as to get a team composite picture. This is a way of getting your team involved in thinking about team building and the great variety of Teamwork Grid® style patterns that characterize different teams as well as in examining the likelihood that there may be more team potential available among your members than you ever realized or even dreamed.

Once these data are summarized it affords a natural opportunity to sit down with your team and begin to draw out what they mean. The way of doing it is identical with the way that has been pictured.

But there are additional angles that can be examined in a fruitful way. Depending on how you have the data summarized, you may have them organized so as to emphasize individual differences in how each member saw each Teamwork Grid® style. That can be done either by specific scales or in a composite that pictures the Teamwork Grid® style itself. The advantage of this is that when done so, wide discrepancies between the top number assigned to a scale or a Teamwork Grid® style invite explanation, particularly when the bottom number is far different. Then if each person feels free to explain why he or she evaluated the team as was done, a very natural basis is provided for beginning to discuss teamwork.

If things have gone well thus far, your next step might be to lead a discussion within the team of whether or not they and you might find it beneficial and rewarding to engage in team building in a manner similar to that described in Chapter 11. A way of doing this would be not to ask for a decision at this time but to ask people to read Chapter 11 and think about what the implications of doing team building might be for your own team, with your mentioning that the decision can be made in the next week, 10 days, or 2 weeks after each person has had a full opportunity to read Chapter 11 and beyond, as well as to ponder the implications of doing team building in this team.

What follows is a way of aiding you in thinking through the pros and cons of getting your team involved in team building. Note that it might be worthwhile to reexamine your judgments for any possibility of self-deception, particularly if the 9,9 score is between 84 and 108 as your dominant team style.

This assessment should provide you with a picture of the current state of your team and its opportunities for change. Two issues emerge: (1) Does teamwork need improvement? and (2) How can team building be approached?

Does Your Teamwork Need Improvement?

The need for improvement stems from the leadership and the current culture of the team. Each must support the other; yet each can limit the other. Leadership, for example, can range from domineering to impoverished. As a result, team members in a 9,1 team culture may earnestly desire participation but they may be excluded or overpowered. At the other end is the 1,1 team; it is impoverished by neglect and loss of member involvement. Paternalism extracts compliance in exchange for benefits, praise, and absence of criticism — but it fails to integrate the views of the team members. Similar generalizations, but each pointing in its own unique direction, can be made for the opportunistic, 1,9-, 5,5-, or 9,9-oriented teams.

Nevertheless, sound, well-intended leadership may still be unable to overcome an established level of norms and standards that have grown up as the "operating rules" of the team. It becomes very difficult—even for an able leader—to confront established expectations and elicit participation without resentment. It is only when the leader and members gain an accurate assessment of the current condition and contrast it with a desirable future condition that needed changes become apparent to all. Under these circumstances, change can be effected without resentment.

Accurate diagnosis can sharpen the issues and determine whether the impediments to effective teamwork are in the exercise of leadership or in the extant team culture.

Solo diagnosis can be misleading. A leader, like anyone else, can fall into the trap of self-delusion and decide the problem is the team. Subordinates can conclude that the problem is one of leadership. Collective diagnosis, where team members undertake the analysis as a group, is subject to the same influences that distort regular teamwork.

One of the interesting observations these authors have made from their review of team self-assessment is the "six" dynamic. When teams rate themselves on 9-point scales, it is rare for any evaluation to fall below 6. Indeed, there is such a concentration at the level 6, and such avoidance of ratings below 6, as to deny any statistically rational explanation.

It follows that a behavioral explanation needs to be sought, and we conclude that pride in membership of even the most impoverished team leads members to limit their critical evaluations. No one really wants to admit to being an active participant in failure; no one really wants to stand out so negatively as to repel his or her teammates and deny the possibility of future cooperation.

How Can Team Building Be Approached?

The answer to the dilemma of achieving an accurate analysis of team performance lies in adopting high standards of diagnosis. If anyone in the team — leader or other member — senses an attraction to an unacceptable style or a shortfall from the ideal, it is probably worth exploring team building, the systematic examination of team performance against desired standards and formulation of strategies to elevate performance. The business world is just too unforgiving to risk the possibility of a shortfall in team effectiveness.

If the primary indexes of team performance — that is, productivity, creativity, and satisfaction — are not fulfilled, there is even further evidence of the need for change. The outcome of a systematic team building effort should reflect the current performance level of the team. If a team is already effective, it will welcome refinements that further hone its high standards. If a team has problems, a specific change program is an indispensable mechanism for identifying and facing up to them.

Teams may undertake team building efforts in a variety of ways. For some it is possible to engage in development activities on their own, with no outside assistance. More typically some form of outside help is relied on to provide guidance and direction. The two examples provided earlier in Figure 9.2 demonstrate this.

As can be seen from the ratings, Team 1 is evaluated as having a high degree of the 9,9 team culture in contrast to the other possibilities. If these ratings had been an accurate description of this team before they undertook team building, it was probably operating effectively enough to pursue team building activities on its own, without the assistance of a consultant. Such a team is likely to have participation skills and a degree of openness and candor that enable them to further strengthen areas where they are less than fully effective. In Team 2 we find that a 9,1 team culture has developed. In such a situation it is less likely that the team can successfully move into team building activities on its own. Should they attempt to do so, it might lead to the boss using the opportunity to solidify control. If there is a norm of win–lose infighting among team members, they might engage in a contest of wills to see who can prevail. In either event, it is likely to require an outsider to confront the boss and the other members about their objectives and how their behavior is counterproductive to team performance.

Given the desirability of team building as a consolidative or a corrective mechanism, the next decision is what approach to use. Theory-based team building is detailed in Chapter 11 and five alternatives to this approach are reviewed in Chapters 12 and 13.

Chapter Ten

How to Bring It About

M ost people readily admit that strengthening teamwork is important and needed. In reality, however, most organizations do not undertake team building, and few know what to do about it. Some organizations are caught up in the rush of day-to-day business, others do not wish to upset the status quo, and still others become complacent when they gain an advantage over competitors.

In today's rapidly changing business environment avoiding or ignoring the need for increased teamwork effectiveness invites a number of risks. One is that the team and its members are insulated from changes going on about them. Another risk is that the present but outmoded cultural norms continue to dominate business decisions. Participation skills may remain inadequate. When adjustments are attempted, the same attitudes and processes that created the current state of the team come into play to resist or dilute the change efforts. Simple desire for improvement in teamwork is not likely to be adequate to sustain a change effort. Some action to break the cycle is imperative.

Participation Skills

Conventional wisdom suggests that effectiveness comes from a strong leader, a clear mission, and technically competent subordinates. Yet more is involved if a team is to realize synergy. The key issue is in how the parts act together — participation. It is the core issue of productivity, creativity, and satisfaction. If participation is withheld or discouraged, then some of the resources of the team remain untapped. Even more important, lack of participation denies the potential of emergent solutions — those which no one grasps at the onset but which may be drawn out from the resolution of conflicting positions.

However, even the desire to participate or to have participation is not enough. Participation involves team members acquiring a set of skills. More often than not those skills may be weak or subordinated by longtime experience in an inhibiting culture. One can imagine a young person with a burning desire to drive a car. The desire may be there, but a set of skills must be learned to move successfully from desire to realization. Having been a passenger may be helpful but to actively participate as a driver in today's busy traffic requires far more than "having watched." There are occasional examples of teams who are "born again" in the sense that they come to a sharper realization of where they are and where they want to be and have the skills to do so. However, the probability of a smooth transition becomes greatly enhanced by a systematic, theory-based approach to participation skills.

Similarly, a member of a team may be convinced of the need for change and have a genuine desire to move toward a more productive and desirable team culture. Then, two points become established — what the team is like now and what it wants to become. What remains is to shift from one to the other by using a process and conducting that process in a sound manner. The process is team building. Its soundness as an approach to change is contingent on the development of membership skills requisite for effective participation. These are essential for an effective transition from the current state to the desired or ideal state.

Effective participation results in a greater flow of ideas and positions and requires a sound means to deal with the differences that emerge. As a team tackles the handling of more information and more conflict, skills of efficient processing become essential. The following items reflect team-work when participation skills are highly developed.

- The team atmosphere is such that it welcomes input or challenges those who have none.
- Input is presented thoroughly and clearly.
- Listening skills give attention to the input to register and acknowledge it.
- Discussion is open with elastic collisions of ideas that leave the participants "undented" by rejection of their ideas for logical reasons.
- Decisions are rational and based on facts to achieve understanding and commitment.
- Emotions are recognized as vital and legitimate elements of social exchange.
- Candor is high in order to permit open reaction.
- Critique is exercised to understand what is occurring and to shift the character or content of discussion if needed.

The list may seem overwhelming, but with a theory base for understanding these concepts and with practice in their use, this kind of teamwork becomes natural.

Identifying Team Participation Skills

The model of team participation skills includes the following.

Decision Making

Sound team decision making means that facts, data, and logic are relied on in coming to understanding and agreement. It does not mean that rank or status of individual members is the determining factor, that the person with the loudest voice prevails, or that majority rule or pressure tactics are required for decision making. Team members support decisions when remaining doubts and reservations have been resolved.

Objectives

Team members have clear goals and objectives toward which they strive. Then activities for getting there have purpose and direction. Rather than simply working within the status quo, doing what they are told, or repeating yesterday, they know specifically what the team is trying to achieve. As a result, members are likely to make better contributions and to find greater gratification from doing so.

Coordination

Good coordination is evident when team members demonstrate the capacity to mesh effort and accomplish objectives in a valid, timely, and interdependent way, even under pressure for results.

Communication

Clear and candid communication among members is essential for an exchange of facts, feelings, and points of view. Solutions reached can then be of high quality with relevant issues discussed factually and with candor.

Critique

Team-centered critique of the quality or performance effectiveness being realized is continuous. Being involved in critique means accepting responsibility for sharing with one another thoughts and feelings, reservations and doubts, and hopes and aspirations regarding the interaction process behind present operations so that task accomplishment can be made more effective.

The Case for Participation Training Before Team Building

Although it is possible to incorporate participation training into the actual team building activities themselves, experience has demonstrated that there are distinct advantages to undertaking this training independently of and prior to team building activities. Laying a foundation for participation is a desirable step before trying to build higher performance into a "live" team.

1. Critique skills in many teams are in essentially an unusable form. They need to be upgraded to gain the maximum benefits possible.

2. Experienced-based learning about participation is a stronger basis for acquiring effectiveness than cognitive (reading) or passive (lecture format) methods are.

3. Acquiring a conceptual framework for thinking about and discussing issues of effectiveness is essential if team members are to develop mutual understanding of what constitutes sound teamwork.

4. Candor is a prerequisite for discussing in an open and frank manner real issues of teamwork. Standards of openness and candor are more easily developed in a "neutral" environment where one is free to be candid

without fear of repercussions. They are unlikely to emerge in the actual work team setting unless these standards are shared by all team members.

5. Team members often have difficulty in mustering the courage to tackle the boss in a candid way. Practice in giving and receiving feedback without the boss present helps ensure that any boss-related issues are faced during team building proper.

6. Each team member needs to experience an emotional tip-over from wanting to win his or her own position to the objective of contributing to the best team solution.

7. Learning to handle conflict in a constructive manner is prerequisite to dealing with increased participation and the emergence of candor in the "live" team.

8. Synergy is an intellectually attractive concept, but learning experiences with achieving it strengthen convictions about its desirability and the ability of team members to actually attain it.

9. The decision to move into team building is soundest when it arises from value-based convictions gained through learning about participation rather than coming to a decision based on faith or recommendation.

10. An incubation time between participation training and team building is likely to stimulate and deepen additional insights into the specifics of effective performance.

An obstacle to any self-oriented framework such as the Teamwork Grid® has to be identified and removed before the benefits from participation training can be realized. The barrier is in self-deception, about which a great deal is known and understood. It is the issue Robert Burns recognized in the famous phrase, "O wad some Pow'r the giftie gie us to see oursels as others see us!"

Open and candid colleague feedback is the key to removing self-deception which is present in the form of assessment of one's own Teamwork Grid® style. The data in Table 10.1 show that prior to participation training approximately 60% of managers see their approach to utilizing power and authority as 9,9. After colleague feedback the 9,9 self-assessment is in the neighborhood of 13%, with the 9,1 and 5,5 styles coming into their own, once people have learned to see themselves more objectively. These data confirm that Robert Burns was right on target.

Table 10.1. Changes in Self-Assessment from Managerial Grid Seminar Participation Training.

| | Grid Style % | |
Grid Descriptions	Pre Dominant	Post (after 1 week of colleague feedback) Dominant
9,9	59.8	13.4
9+9	7.7	12.0
9,1	9.4	30.4
5,5	17.2	38.1
1,9	5.7	5.6
1,1	0.2	0.5

These data are based on self-reports by 647 participants.

What to Avoid in Participation Skills Training

One of the purposes of participation training is to free the team from defensiveness or nonproductive reaction to differences of opinion and ideas. Thus courses that teach how to control the situation by assertiveness or situational reaction are more likely to increase defenses than to reduce them. Courses which advocate manipulation are unlikely to promote the emergence of the candor essential for active teamwork. Individual team members react to aggressive or manipulative behavior with distrust, making it more difficult to substitute team-centered commitment for an individual-centered orientation.

Courses that provide techniques for facilitation of meetings or mechanical guidelines for eliciting participation can be helpful, but they are of limited value when stakes are high and the solution to a problem is unclear to all. In these cases resolution of conflicting points of view by mechanical procedures is almost certain to result in a half-a-loaf result.

Regardless of content, courses that attempt to impart participation skills by passive methods such as reading, lecture, and film often fall short of accomplishing their objectives, because without hands-on experience and practice in participation skills the knowledge gained is insufficient or quickly forgotten.

A team operates best using its own internal resources. Training in participation reduces the need for direction or "coaching" by a consultant or other outside expert, which, itself, is unlikely to have the impact on team performance that a self-convincing learning experience of participation can produce.

The Need For Outside Resources

A team convinced of the opportunities of team building might naturally seek outside help. It is only logical to seek expert advice in areas of unfamiliarity. The question is, "Is a consultant really necessary, or can a team lift itself up by its own bootstraps?"

Some teams are already in good shape and enjoy more than their share of synergistic solutions to problems. A team such as the 9,9 team presented in Chapter 8 stands to gain many benefits through engaging in "do it yourself" team building. They may be in a position to take the background thinking discussed in this book and use it to their own gain and without reliance on a consultant to help them.

But certainly this conclusion is not true for all teams. Some teams are in deep trouble with much distrust and mutual recrimination. For them, the likelihood of being able to press the magic button and simply become an outstanding team on a do-it-yourself basis is not in the cards. The 9,1-oriented team described in Chapter 2 is so embedded in a fight culture that if they engaged in team building without outside help, they would only increase the frequency with which members land body punches on one another. Other teams suffer comparable problems such as too much sweetness and light, shared indifference, or status quo complacency.

Is There a Real Need?

Several questions should be considered before the decision is made whether to use a consultant or not.

A need might be perceived in the risk of self-deception and it can be a legitimate concern. A team may feel trapped within its own culture which is so deeply embedded that although members know that theirs is not productive teamwork they persist in repeating it. This can be seen in the difficulty of tackling a strong member or in dealing with a major issue that is in conflict. Many of these issues are within the province of the team and care should be taken to prevent outside help from shoring up a weakness or permitting the team to avoid facing up to the problem.

Is Outside Help Likely to Bring More Baggage?

Consultants come as whole people. It is difficult to hire a part of one and avoid the risk of more input, content, and conflicting theories that may only divert the team from addressing its real needs. Some consultants see their role as highly directional and inadvertently take over the team. The best choice seems to be to avoid such problems entirely if possible or to set expectations that the consultant not become involved in the actual operations of the team.

Will It Create an Ongoing Dependency?

The presence of a consultant may not do the trick either for two reasons: (1) The team may operate as though on its good behavior when the consultant is present but then immediately revert to its old battle lines when the consultant is absent. (2) If the consultant is helpful to members and they come to lean on him or her, it may be that he or she produces dependency reactions and team members come to realize that they can only do well when the consultant is present. This does not solve the team's problem; it only creates more demand for the consultant.

If help is thought to be needed, the choice should be made from among those consultants whose policy it is to help clients help themselves. These consultants build themselves out of the client over the long run rather than creating an ongoing relationship.

There is an even better solution to the consultant problem than having an outside expert to work with every team building activity. When everything is done in a sound manner, it is the top team that does team building first. The reason is that the top team is the leader team in the sense of setting the model for what constitutes effective teamwork for itself and for everyone else. By engaging in team building on a "do as I do" basis rather than "do as I say," teams lower in the organization realize that they are not being asked to do something by way of development that has not already been done by those above them. When the sequence of team building is such that it starts at the top, then it may be desirable to have an outsider present to increase the prospects for success. The consultant's most important contribution is to challenge self-deception in order to aid team members to escape from their actual culture.

After the top team has undertaken team building, there remains little need for additional reliance on outside consultants to help lower-level teams along in team building. Other teams in the organization can benefit from an insider, one who is not a member of the team but is a member of the organization and who has already experienced team building as a member of a higher-level team. Sitting with them as team building is undertaken, he or she can do the same things as an outside consultant might have been called on to do. This process can be repeated as many times as is necessary.

There are several advantages beyond simply avoiding the use of an outside consultant. The internal "resource" person is able to learn more about problems of teamwork by virtue of observing another team, in which he or she is not a member, grapple with such problems. Not being a part of the team, it becomes possible to view these problems in a more neutral and objective manner. This serves to reinforce the convictions of such a resource person about the importance of really grappling in a sound way with impediments to effective teamwork. Another advantage is that an insider serving in the role of a consultant is far less likely to produce dependency. Team members realize that the resource person is not an expert but simply a line or staff person with prior experience in team building who is helping members who have team problems of participation see themselves in more objective terms. Since the resource person is not a part of team problems, he or she can provide an outsider point of view but without producing dependency on the outsider to tell the team what to do.

One disadvantage is that it does take an additional amount of time away from direct work for the insider who serves as the consultant resource person. However, the development contribution of having the opportunity to serve as a team consultant in team building far outweighs the time consideration. Even this expenditure can be minimized by providing that no person be asked to serve as a resource on a steady basis or repeatedly. In this way serving as a team consultant can be experienced by many and, simultaneously, not divert too much time and effort from that person's primary operational responsibilities.

Conclusion

It is possible and certainly an attractive alternative for a team to engage in team building on its own, but to do so successfully warrants some development by members of participation skills before seeking to change a "live" team. The most significant risk of engaging in team building without acquiring participation skills or outside support is the pervasiveness of self-deception in evaluating both personal and team performance. More than good intentions are necessary for most teams if they are to break out of their history by examining their past performance with objectivity and against high standards.

Which Approach To Use

Many different approaches are encompassed in the name of team building. Most feature a programmed sequence of activities that lead the team through a set of learning experiences designed to create convergent thinking and a shared interest in results. Some are freestanding—as a set of materials in written, audiovisual, tape, or combination form. Some require the presence of a consultant or facilitator. Whatever the choice, the focus of concentration of team building programs can be classified into two categories—process-oriented and content-oriented.

Process-Oriented Programs

Process-oriented programs focus on the way in which teams function—the "how" of teamwork. Interventions are utilized in an attempt to break the pattern of culture. As team members gain greater insight into how they are performing, they are able to alter their actions for the better. Often the insight is supplied by an outside expert or facilitator who causes them to discover the impediments to performance by one of several strategies as follows.

An issue of process-oriented development is that four of the five interventions involve resources from outside the team. Theory-based intervention presents the option of acquiring insight through written or other material and the benefit of little or no use of outside resources. Acceptant requires an accepter; catalytic, a catalyst; confrontation, a confronter; prescription, a prescriber.

Theory-based provides a theoretical framework on which the team members can evaluate performance themselves and sort out what is and what appears to be happening. A common conceptual foundation and language forms a basis for greater insight and ability to communicate without the cumbersome semantics of behavioral description.

Acceptant takes the form of nondirective counseling. Team activities are probed with leading questions but no input. In the process of responding team members gain insight into their own action and motives and the effect it has on others.

Catalytic is similar to acceptant, but input is added in the form of suggestions and tentative conclusions, all aimed at relieving the tensions that otherwise disrupt performance.

Confrontational features a confrontation of the differences between the facts and the perceived situation. Teams and members are forced to face up to differences between their intentions and the actual results of their actions.

Prescriptive is when teams or members are told what to do to better performance. Acceptability of the prescription is derived from expert judgment. Prescriptions are often "safe" and take the form of equipment, location, or organizational changes, avoiding the behavorial dimensions that may be the real cause of inadequacy.

Content-Oriented Programs

Content-oriented programs take as their focal issue the strengthening of some topic to which teams apply their energies to the nuts and bolts of the business. They are concerned with the "what" of team activity. Topics such as quality, excellence, or communication become the rallying point for discussion. The commonality of the subject leads team members into collective pursuit of a shared objective. In the process, team members are induced to work with each other in a coordinated way. Differences are expected to become subordinated as team members discover the rewards of mutual effort.

The attraction of content programs is the near-term benefit of accomplishing some high-profile result. The disadvantage is that cultural norms are likely to be little affected. For example, it is possible to complete such a program under any Teamwork Grid® style team culture—9,1 authoritarian; 1,9 warm, winning approval; 5,5 staying in step; 1,1 indifference by going through the paces; and so on. Content programs often falter on unhealthy culture; for example, the design can be rigorously followed but implementation founders on low commitment.

Content programs offer many benefits, but a better sequence provides for team building first and then pursuit of whatever nuts and bolts issues are important. The logic is that a soundly operating team will have fewer problems in completing a content program and implementing it through to the desired results. Probably the worst shortfall of content programs is that of creating the illusion of teamwork progress while the real issues remain untouched.

Conclusion

A theory-based, process skills-oriented approach appears best in addressing the real barriers and in placing responsibility for outcomes with the team. It faces the issues and avoids the potential of creating dependency on a consultant or a facilitator for future effectiveness.

Examples of the different approaches are dealt with in the following chapters with emphasis placed on theory-based, process-oriented team building.

Chapter Eleven

A Light at the End of the Tunnel

*You cannot help men permanently by doing for them
what they could and should do for themselves*
—Abraham Lincoln

The theory-based approach to team building is one in which all management team members learn the theories of individual and collective behavior, as illustrated in Chapters 2 through 8, before team building is undertaken.

Because behavior is driven by the attitudes and assumptions individuals hold about the best way to manage, understanding one's own managerial assumptions can facilitate (1) an intellectual decision to replace practices that may be impeding or otherwise adversely affecting team performance and (2) an increase in the participation skills that are essential for excellent teamwork.

The dimensions of teamwork illustrated by the scales at the end of Chapters 2 through 8 and reproduced later in the Appendix are the following:

1. Power and authority
   (Items 1, directions and 2, meetings)
2. Structure and differentiation
   (Items 7, job descriptions and 8, delegation)
3. Norms and standards
   (Items 9, quality and 3, conflict)
4. Goals and objectives
   (Items 4, objectives and 5, innovation)
5. Feedback and critique
   (Items 10, performance appraisals and 6, communication)
6. Morale and cohesion
   (Items 11, team spirit and 12, commitment)

These must be addressed in a succession of team building activities designed to produce a model or ideal, compare it with current practices, and establish the differences between them as a basis for planned change.

Thus the consultant, if needed at all, acts as a resource. He or she only intervenes as necessary to ensure that the issues are addressed in an atmosphere of open communication. The consultant's objective is to make the team self-sufficient and self-correcting. Responsibility for success remains with the team.

When teamwork development is pursued in this systematic way, uniformly positive results can be expected. The team members themselves are the carriers of the team culture. They have the opportunity to change behavior based on insight rather than edict, compromise, or some other method that cannot elicit commitment to real change. Sound theory provides a framework for comparing both sound and unsound approaches to teamwork and for predicting the consequences of less effective teamwork.

The teamwork development plan is designed to provide direction while being flexible enough to deal with unique problems. One of its goals is to avoid regression to previous ways of operations. Another goal is highlighting the gaps between what the team members believe to be sound operating procedure and the way they are actually operating. This creates a strong motivation for positive change and willingness and enthusiasm to carry it forward.

Carter entered the conference room accompanied by Jeff Robertson. Jeff stood aside as Carter greeted his management team. Then Carter turned to his guest.

CARTER: Jeff, I would like to introduce you to my management. You've met Joe Segal who heads personnel. He suggested this meeting.

Ed Simmons heads finance; Richard Smalley, production; Jim Anderson, consumer marketing; Betty Johnson, product development; and Luther Thompson, original equipment marketing. We sell extensively to other manufacturers — automotive and the like. Please, take this seat here beside me.

I've asked Jeff to come here today to talk to us about his experience in his own company. They have mounted a major development program and it may have some bearing on what we may wish to do.

As you know, I've sent Joe Segal around our company looking for areas of superior performance and he has been wandering around and conveying my interests in excellence. He's found one area that he believes is superior. I call it a "pocket of excellence." It's characterized by high achievement and high motivation and stands out from the rest of us. You might even call it spectacular teamwork. Joe Segal and Richard Smalley were the architects of Flat Creek and Peter Burnside was the builder. I think you all know that story.

I know that the rest of you may be disappointed that your divisions do not seem yet to meet that standard of excellence. But that is why we are here. Joe Segal and I have tried to encourage others to follow the Flat Creek example. Peter Burnside has been open and helpful, but even he had difficulties in spreading it to Gardenvale. Apparently teams don't pick up clues about how to do it from teams that have reached a plane of excellence and I'm in a quandary as to why because I have offered them every encouragement. About all I can do right now is quote the King of Siam to Anna, "It's a puzzlement."

The strange phenomenon is that we really don't know how to get a pocket of excellence started, or how to cross-fertilize one success to another. It seems that change doesn't happen by osmosis.

I wanted to make some very candid observations today even though I realize they may be a bit embarrassing and I apologize for that. But I think we need to see the picture as clearly as possible.

Jeff, I heard some splendid things from Joe Segal about the effort you have been spearheading in your company. We would appreciate your telling us of what you are doing. Can you shed any light on our efforts?

JEFF: Well, thank you, Bill. I'm not sure how you got me into this. And I'm certainly no expert. But I can tell you what we are doing and the basis for it. Then perhaps we can open the discussion. That might be more profitable.

To begin with, we followed much the same course of trying to get people to learn from one another by the "osmosis approach." And we had much the same frustration at spotty results. We felt we only really knew how to make success happen when we found a theory base for strengthening teamwork; individual effort was not enough, no matter how vigorous.

Learning how to grapple with team culture was the key for us. We made progress when we were ready to face up to our culture and jointly decided to work toward a better one. That was the breakthrough that earned our commitment. We call it "change by design."

JOE: Pete Collins, who is one of our new plant human resource managers, has been talking about norms, silent rules that everyone salutes unknowingly. Is that it?

JEFF: Yes. An individual has difficulty breaking out of team norms. It can only take place when all members together think through and reject existing norms before committing themselves to different ones. For that to happen, it has to be a joint decision. It can't happen merely by the boss saying, "I want this or that to take place."

RICHARD: How do you explain Flat Creek?

JEFF: I don't know. From what I understand, it was a new team and they created their own new culture under good leadership. I suspect there's a great deal more than that to their story.

BETTY: What do I do about my product development department? They've all been building empires for themselves.

JEFF: Exactly the point. You'll have difficulty effecting change. It's group pressure. Norms that are in place create resistance to change.

CARTER: The thing about our examples is that they're different from the overall. What's our overall culture?

JIM: That's a good point. But a systemwide change has to start at the top. Why not concentrate on this team? This is the company we all know and we can begin to try to answer the question based on our own experience.

CARTER: Does that make sense?

JEFF: Yes, it does. The top is where the action starts. People who work together should be able to talk freely. That's essential.

RICHARD: Bill, you asked what's our culture. I think I'm ready to tell you. You're a good man. You try to help us. But you "manage" us. You give the orders and expect us to jump. Not that you haven't a big heart. We all know and appreciate your trying to look after each of us. But you treat us like a father treats a child. We'll never learn how to ride a bicycle with your hand on the back of the seat.

LUTHER: I think he's right. For example, the project that Joe Segal has been on is your way of saying, "I'm for excellence and I want to commend the effort to get excellence to every manager in this company," but somehow it didn't come through as a challenge that we pick up. We've been saluting it all right, but that's about all.

ED: I think that is unfair . . . Mr. Carter has given his life to this company.

BETTY: I think I see a lot of saluting that covers up inertia throughout a lot of this company.

CARTER: I'm to blame for all this?

JOE: No, but you're part of it. If Jeff's right, we're all to blame.

JEFF: There's no one to blame, and there's everyone to blame. It's the situation that grew. Top leadership has a big influence, but you all let it happen. What's important is to find out what to do now, set some new standards, involve the others, and develop some shared basis for team culture.

JOE: How did you get your company to face up?

JEFF: The steps were simple. We felt we needed a theory base and we knew we had to develop a common language. We chose a seminar for doing that because it provided good ideas about how to deal with the conflicts that would crop up as we tried to introduce change. Without some common language and concepts we probably would have been thrown back to square one.

Then we moved into team building. It took three or four days for each team to use critique to get to a high level of candor but it was the best investment we ever made.

CARTER: What did you do in team building?

JEFF: We decided on the culture we wanted to have. After establishing the "soundest" culture we would like to have, we identified what actually was going on. That comparison gave us a gap we could make plans to close.

We reviewed how we divided up the work. Then we talked about interpersonal barriers, petty things that can hamper a team. But it was only when we began to strip away the self-deception that everyone seemed to carry around in his or her mental luggage that we were able to get straight with one another.

After clearing away this underbrush, we studied the way we set and met objectives and how we should change. We set out a model project, a meaningful job of work to be done by the team in an ideal way. Before long that model became our standard. We haven't looked back.

CARTER: Did the team really level with you?

JEFF: They offered me wise counsel as to how I might strengthen my exercise of leadership. That was sobering but otherwise rewarding.

JOE: That sounds pretty much like what they did at Flat Creek.

CARTER: I didn't realize that was what they did at Flat Creek, but does that give us two points on the curve? Flat Creek has been successful and Jeff has been successful as well.

It was as though a new source of energy had been tapped and the next two hours of lively discussion covered details and procedures. The meeting ended on a positive note—with concrete suggestions for implementing a plan and another meeting set up for the following day.

The First Steps Toward Team Building

The team met several times over the next few weeks. Good progress was made in opening up the issues but in the end they decided they needed a more structured approach in order to deal with the changes effectively. As a first step all team members attended a seminar to learn a common theory base and heighten their participation skills. Joe Segal was asked to look into the outside resources available. Segal called in a consultant whom Jeff Robertson had utilized in the early stages.

CARTER: You're saying that the best location for this team-building task is right where the team works?

BOB ARDEN, CONSULTANT: That's right, and you need several very full days. You might even want to start the afternoon before if you want to handle it without night work.

CARTER: And this material goes out several weeks in advance?

BOB: Right. There's something like 15 hours of prework for each team member, including reading this book. They should have lots of time to think it through.

CARTER: And you say I'm supposed to run these sessions. What are you for?

BOB: I guess you'd say I am a resource—somebody to turn to if the team gets stuck. I also introduce some Teamwork

Grid® theory along the way and challenge you if there's a significant departure. The material's pretty clear, but, like any process, there's a need for quality control.

CARTER: Most other consultants led us by the hand.

BOB: That's not how we operate. The real responsibility for success is yours. If I create a position in the team or any sort of dependency, what happens when I leave?

CARTER: Good point. Joe, have you got all this down?

JOE: I think you should present this to the team—maybe tomorrow. It would be a natural follow-up to our discussions with Jeff Robertson.

CARTER: Maybe. These are just logistics. We do have agreement to go ahead.

BOB: As you look over the material, you'll see there's an early activity where you seek agreement to proceed. Even though you've already decided, it's pretty important to continue to ensure commitment and to explore reservations you or the others may have. If a team-building session doesn't have good support, it's likely to fall short of getting full value. But that's not unlike anything else you plan to do as a group. People are in a better position to judge once they've reviewed the material.

Carter followed the advice and arranged for prework. The team met to explore any reservations members had. There were some but they seemed to fall away as they were brought out into the open. They decided to proceed and were now well into the first of the three days they had reserved.

The theory review and critique had gone well and Carter was pleased as he opened the activity concerned with describing the ideal culture. The prework had included a forced choice instrument that called for individual ranking of various statements from most ideal to least. The atmosphere was now sufficiently open that people had no reluctance to call out how they had completed the Ideal Ranking. Carter recorded these on a flip chart. The first item considered was Directions. It was apparent as the choices were declared that there was a consensus on soundest: "Clear instructions for carrying out responsibilities are provided with opportunity available to clarify unclear areas; everyone understands what is to be done and why it is important."

A brief review of the rationale for the best way was interspersed with quips, with someone saying, "Understand, I didn't say that's what we do; only what we should be doing." Others nodded in an understanding way, with the point being experienced by all that the gap between what actually goes on and what would be truly sound was of considerable width and that important changes would be required to get to the conditions under which the team could mobilize resources to the fullest.

The other alternatives were arrayed in a comparable manner; there was wide agreement that the statement, "directions are minimal; action is based mostly on doing things ritually or one thing at a time as new demands arise," should be ranked as the most unsound. The amount of agreement as to the location of the other alternatives was not as clear, and yet the trends were evident, indicating that members had a good understanding of the issues and what is at stake in terms of team effectiveness when the best alternative is abandoned and some other option takes its place.

The remaining 11 of the instruments were dealt with in a comparable manner. Finally a summary was completed showing that 9,9 was seen to be the sound alternative throughout all 12 of the questions; with 1,1 the most rejected Teamwork Grid® style and the remaining alternatives arrayed between them in the following sequence: paternalism, 9,1, 5,5, 1,9, and opportunism.

The ideal culture activity was the breakthrough. As the ideal became clearer to the team, so did the actual paternalistic nature of the company. Joe Segal and Jim Anderson led much of the thinking in suggesting ways that results could be achieved through shared understanding of purpose. One by one the team gave its support.

The team had a new atmosphere to it. Carter was leading, but not directing. The team was working well. Only Ed Simmons and Luther Thompson were anxious as they discussed the actual situation relative to directions. They could not resist saying so.

LUTHER: Bill, we built this company on a control basis. The statement, "the boss determines the activities to be accomplished and how they are to be done; members are treated well and compliance is expected in everyone's best interest," is the best fit. Over the years we've held the reins. At the same time, we treated people right. This may not be ideal, but I don't see why we should abandon a winning formula-for-success.

JOE: Are there any facts to support that judgment? I see a lot of troubled areas from where I sit. I look at our turnover, our union relationship, and our ability to attract top talent. What did *you* have in mind, Ed?

ED: I don't think we have success, Luther. The numbers don't show it. I'm just an old-fashioned accountant. I'm talking bottom line, cash flow, asset base—things like that.

As the examples flowed, Carter began to realize how reasonable the reactions were. Richard Smalley reviewed a previous proposal to introduce microcomputers which had been met with extreme demands for cost justification. Carter realized he had been too demanding.

The discussion continued and the group agreed that their culture did not allow room for innovation or subordinate's ideas. Not only was it the case in Carter's team; each was doing it to subordinates. Once the group understood their culture they moved on to talk about ways to make it better.

The talk continued — thoughtful, open talk. Carter was patient and supportive. Their review of job descriptions dealt with the way responsibilities were broken out and "territories" came to be decided. Betty Johnson's concern for her group's isolation and self-interest became a team concern as they all began to realize how little real involvement they had in product development's direction.

BETTY: We should really examine current assignments. Better access to specialists would help every one of our operating departments. If, for example, we assigned a contact person from product development for each, we could become much more informed about the company's needs. That would be a good step toward better service.

LUTHER: We just haven't looked at our organization in today's light. Many of our bigger meetings groups just soak up time. We could pair off in subsets of this team to meet a special problem and add one or two specialists if we must. It would be marvelous training for some of our new up and coming talent.

Joe Segal jumped in at that and soon a conflict developed over the priority of training. They struggled for 10 minutes before Bob Arden, the consultant, suggested a critique.

"By George," interjected Carter, "we sure do need some practice. We're quick to fall into old ways."

The critique brought forth a reappraisal, and a new solution, stronger than either of the points around which the battle had ranged, emerged.

Finally Luther spoke up: "You know, if all our meetings were like this one, I think it would surely be worthwhile. Maybe boss control isn't the best answer.

JOE: I think it's the culture we set and only we can change it. Pete Collins introduced me to the idea of norms. Only we can change our own norms. Bill can't — not all alone, anyway.

The group turned to the next item which was objectives. There was some trepidation as people began to discuss each other's job performance and the opportunities for improvement. Feedback came slowly at first, but as candor grew the tensions eased. Suggestions for change were constructive and helpful. Each team member listened carefully and made notes.

Eventually, the sessions concluded but not before the data were summarized and a good discussion of the implications of what had been learned had taken place, with agreement reached that they had been operating according to a paternalistic Teamwork Grid® style. The most disturbing conclusion was that their paternalism had been a turn off to innovation and that the erosion of "bottom line, cash flow, asset base — things like that" reflected the price being paid from embracing paternalism and earning loyalty, obedience, and dependency rather than involvement, commitment, creativity, and innovation.

At the end everyone was eager to carry team building down to their own teams—but they decided to wait until they were confident of their own progress. There were a lot of action steps. A model project was selected and a forward date, some three months later, set for review.

Two areas were chosen for the model project and the inter-relationship between them really made them one. They concluded that the ideal approach, delegation, was the only hope of enlarging feelings of shared responsibility. One way to go about doing it was through encouraging innovation and readiness to experiment, proving to one another that each was ready to mobilize resources below them. The selection of the project itself stood as evidence of the readiness to engage in improved creativity and innovation through experimentation.

They did another thing, however, equally valuable. They forced themselves to decide how they would have done it "the old way." In talking through attitudes toward innovation, for example, they agreed with one another that they do give lip-service approval to innovation. When new ideas are actually brought to the surface, they are greeted with approval but quickly get put on the back burner and, as a result, it is widely recognized that they are not welcome.

They also agreed that if they were doing this project as they had done in the past, they would continue to tighten reins on subordinates at the moment that expectations were not met rather than trying to diagnose whether or not past assignments had been fully thought out. They would not have investigated whether sufficient time had been made available, or whether resources had been insufficient—whatever might have been the explanation other than simply presuming that subordinates had failed to "measure up."

By agreeing on their attitudes toward innovation and delegation, they were able to compare past actions and what needed to be done in order to stimulate innovation in the future. They were able to clearly identify what each needed to do in the future that they had not been doing, and what each had been doing in the past that should no longer be continued.

Overview

The theory-based approach to team building gives each member insight into and practice in the participative skills needed to address the real issues of concern to the team. Adequate opportunity to air reservations and doubts is provided during the session discussing the agreement to proceed. Any questions are talked through to resolution.

As each activity in the procedure unfolds, the team deals with successively more demanding subjects — what should be the ideal culture, what is the "actual," and where change is needed. Finally a short-term project is designed to contribute to the bottom-line results. The ideas and changes that flow from the discussion of each item feed forward to provide an inventory of potential projects. Thus the choice of a project is from the thinking of the entire team and not an individual response to a personally perceived problem. Programmed and spontaneous critique ensures ongoing correction and commitment. The consultant's role is a subordinate one that responds to deadlocks or quality departures. Input is restricted to exceptions. Thus part of the consultant's function is aiding the team to use critique and to think and act independently. Bob Arden's contribution throughout the team building was limited to triggering critique when the team got hung up. In this way members themselves came to realize that the only surefire way to get on top of a hang-up was for them to turn away from the content being discussed and concentrate on the process difficulties in order to resolve them. This new feature became a natural part of team discussions thereafter.

This approach serves to give the team useful practices in teamwork and participation. In summary, the theory-based approach provides a model for any other major effort the team may want to undertake.

Chapter Twelve

The Content Approach to Team Building

One of the most prevalent team building approaches is the adoption of a content issue around which to focus team effort. Frequently, a popular text such as *The Pursuit of Excellence* becomes the focus of the change. The team feels that the "latest techniques" will give them some relative advantage.

Most of the themes are sound. It would be hard to argue against excellence, quality, or productivity as worthy objectives. The common pursuit of an objective also has value. It brings effort into the coordination and holds team members accountable for results. The weakness lies in the neglect of process with the result that:

1. Weak participation skills may persist.
2. Norms are addressed only in the subject areas.
3. Power and authority remain as before in all the untouched areas.
4. A sense of complacency grows from the perception that the team is engaged in a development effort.
5. Self-delusion leaves the real issues — productivity, creativity, and satisfaction — only partially addressed.

Failed quality circles, unfulfilled objectives and long lists of unaddressed recommendations for excellence all lend credence to the principle that sound content cannot successfully be grafted onto unsound team culture. The following is an example of what often happens.

David Holmes, the human resources director, frowned as he cradled the telephone. The call from the president, Steve Bannermann, held an uncharacteristic note of frustration. He picked up the corporate entrepreneurship file, and headed for Steve's office.

John Gabrowski, vice president of administration, was already there when David arrived. There were thick files open in front of each man.

STEVE: Come in and sit down, David. We need your help. (David took his seat, still a little puzzled by the sudden invitation and now a little more so by the anxiety in the air.) David, it's the Corporate Entrepreneurship Program. We've created a monster. It's driving us into the ground. I know how much effort you have put into it but we can't seem to turn the corner.

DAVID: Turn the corner?

STEVE: Yes. Since the task forces got underway they've turned out an average of two reports a week and we can't seem to handle the issues.

The time we're spending on this program is just becoming too costly to the ongoing operation. I'm really at a loss. Our executive committee has met three times as a steering group. We have cleared six items. There are 14 pages of items and more coming in. At this rate, we're just not keeping up to the task forces—and that doesn't count all the background rationale and other content of the reports.

DAVID: We can't quit now, Steve. There's too much enthusiasm out there.

STEVE: I know, David. That's why I called for your help. The log jam is in the executive committee. We just can't seem to come to a decision. Can we get someone in to help? Have you got any ideas?

DAVID: Well, I don't understand why we should be having a problem, Steve. We decided that this program would be useful. We all read the book. We had the author in for two days. I remember that one — I paid the bill out of the human resources' budget. We had deep discussions. We reviewed the case histories of corporate entrepreneurship. What's the real problem?

JOHN: It's territory wars. No one will concede. Everyone seems to take each suggestion as a personal intrusion on his own management creativity.

DAVID: I thought this program would unify us around a common goal. It certainly has signs of that in lower levels. We even have the union with us in this one.

STEVE: Good Lord, have we got a bear by the tail!

DAVID: Steve, you'll just have to make the decisions and move us on.

STEVE: And ride roughshod over my executives? You of all people should know better than that.

DAVID: Well, Steve, what are the alternatives?

STEVE: That's exactly why I called you. Right now the alternatives seem to be an end with horror or an horror without end. . . .

DAVID: As I see it, this program has almost the same characteristics of the quality circles effort of four years ago. It was a sound target but we failed in the implementation. When the expectations of the organization were violated, it turned everybody off.

Steve, I think the problem is teamwork — or the lack of it. I had hoped this program would force our hand — or yours. The idea of entrepreneurship is imaginative and compelling; it should force us to adopt good working relationships to bring it about.

STEVE: Are you saying you deliberately led us into a swamp?

DAVID: Not really. You made the decision from the book you read on an airplane, Steve. I told you it would be tough, but worth it if we could carry it off. Now we either have to spike the program or face our team and corporate culture and change it.

JOHN: Steve, Dave's right. It was your program and it is time we faced up. We may have to delay the program, but, if we can open up our executive committee, it may well be worth more than the program itself.

Steve's anger mounted. A pulse showed at his temples. The other two men waited for his response.

Rationale

The foregoing dialogue describes a problem typical of this approach. The lack of participative skills and a collision of program values with organizational values have created a stalemate. Should the program be allowed to continue in an unfavorable environment or should a favorite cause, in which a great deal of effort has been invested, be abandoned?

Another example might be the introduction of MBO (management by objectives). Management by objectives which rests on subordinates' participating in their own objective setting, is a classic example from the past when the value systems of the MBO technique frequently were incongruent with the value systems of the organization. Many authoritarian managers embraced MBO as a control mechanism to enforce further compliance. Subordinates, who generally rejected the notion of further control, went through the motions without commitment.

Theory Z and quality circles often failed for the same sort of reason. Programs of a highly participative nature tend to derive their success from personal commitment rather than knuckled-under compliance. Productivity and quality programs often suffer the same strains of contradiction of values.

Content programs are invaluable to teams that have worked through their cultural problems and have developed a sense of the need for involvement and participation. But they are not effective in trying to improve a troubled team. The additional burden of a content program is more likely to exacerbate problems than to cure them.

Chapter Thirteen

Process Approaches to Building a Team

A t this point you probably sense that barriers to effective teamwork are numerous, widespread, and persistent. Recognition of this fact led to a series of experiments a few years ago in which first steps were taken into team building. Team building means taking deliberate action to identify and remove barriers to effective teamwork and to replace them with the kind of sound behavior that can lead to superlative performance.

Since those early experiments there has been much concentrated effort by many people to find the "best" way to build teams. Five different models emerged from their efforts. In picturing them, think of yourself as a consultant who works with the team to help it identify, remove, and replace whatever barriers to teamwork exist within that group. The five models are summarized in this chapter.

The Acceptant or Nondirective Approach

This approach is based on the recognition that:

1. Every team member is frustrated at one time or another.
2. People often have less than ample opportunity to air their feelings toward the team or toward its members.

As time goes on, members build walls around themselves and the team develops habits of conduct to stay away from tender topics.

The acceptant or nondirective approach is aimed at solving these types of problems. Here, a consultant's role is to enable members to express their feelings in a reflective way. Each team member is helped:

1. To learn what emotional reactions he or she produces in others

2. To express his or her feelings about others

The objective is to heal emotional tensions that exist within a team.

The acceptant approach often has the positive effect of bringing people closer to one another and of promoting cohesion and high morale. On the negative side, however, this approach runs the risk of focusing on human relations as the perceived target outcome. While the catharsis of candor is likely to relieve built-up tensions, it is unlikely that the team will discuss productivity issues.

Another weakness in this approach is the creation of a consultant dependency. Since the consultant is the agent of change, the team develops a reliance on that agent, rather than developing its own participation skills.

The following is a typical example of acceptant intervention.

"Frankly, I'm worried about the course of our team."

Paul Sanderson, the marketing vice president, looked up at these words from his sales manager. Jack Peterson never seemed worried about anything. It was unusual for him to express concern—and the idea for a team development project was his in the first place. Jack continued, "I think this place runs on hard-line control. It's built into us. Now everyone is full of vague fears about the possible consequences of this effort. People feel they'll lose their present prestige and control unless they can clearly see how this action will enhance control."

PAUL: What do you think we should do, Jack?

JACK: Well, I remember a consultant who ran encounter groups back about four years ago. I think he might be able to help us.

Paul thought for a moment and then replied, "Well, if you think it will help us break out, why don't you get your friend in."

Jack did some telephoning and two weeks later had assembled the team to meet the consultant.

Don Farley, the consultant, stood at the flip charts as he completed his introduction. The team had listened attentively, but there were no questions. Farley sat down at the circular table now ringed with curious faces.

Farley began, "We all have weaknesses that cover our real feelings. That's only human. We can't help that. As long as feelings remain hidden, we can't relate to each other in an open, effective way. Perhaps we should start by sharing our weaknesses. As your consultant I'll start off by telling you mine. . . ."

Four weeks went by. Each Thursday, the team met under Farley's guidance. Their discussions became open, even intimate. Private reservations were disclosed. Motives were out in the open. But Paul was dissatisfied as he reviewed the process with Jack.

PAUL: Jack, I don't think we're getting anywhere.

JACK: What makes you think that?

PAUL: Well, we can't seem to get going. We still can't get the ball into play. We've become humanists but we've lost our drive. If something hurts — even a little — we don't want to handle it.

JACK: Don't you think we've grown as human beings, Paul?

PAUL: No doubt about it. But I want us to grow as good businesspeople. We've become caring, sharing, supportive, even loving. But by damn, this is not what I hoped for in team development. It's all right as a state of being. It feels good. But when I think about the need for a great leap forward, for major improvement in our performance, I'm not satisfied we're on the right track.

JACK: Paul, you wanted participation. We have that.

PAUL: Jack, I wanted participation—participation with action toward a goal. Let's not continue this approach.

JACK: You'll have to discuss it with the team—and the consultant.

PAUL: Yes, I suppose I will.

Rationale

Acceptant change programs run the risk of focus on human relations as the perceived target outcome. Whereas the catharsis of candor is likely to relieve built-up tensions, lack of direction is a prerequisite of acceptant intervention. The likelihood of a team arriving at productivity issues is remote. Although it may be true that even a blind chicken finds a peice of corn, reliance on chance is not enough to ensure sound results.

Another weakness is the creation of a consultant dependency. Since the consultant has been the agent of change, the team develops a reliance on that agent, rather than developing its own participation skills.

It is possible to combine an acceptant intervention to expose and deal with values, followed by a content issue to give direction, but such a course appears contrived: "You get me to lower my guard and then you hit me with a new obligation." The problem of participation skills and consultant dependency remains even if the combination weathers the perception of a contrived outcome.

The Catalytic or Facilitator Approach

A second way of going about team building is giving the consultant more responsibility to interview all team members in private, one after another and/or to administer a questionnaire or some kind of a survey instrument. The answers are summarized and fed back anonymously at a team meeting. The consultant might offer procedural suggestions as to how the team might examine the survey data and judge its implications for team effectiveness. The following vignette is a typical example of a catalytic approach.

George Sampson, the manager of research and development, called the meeting to order. He described his concern with the working relationships of the project teams and how he felt the present circumstances were stifling innovation. He then described how Jack Clark, the consultant, might aid the group to break through the creativity barrier.

Jack Clark started his part of the meeting with a summary of possible causes, which were gleaned from his interviews with each team member. To avoid provoking tensions, Jack put the problem in his own words, and separated the comment from the source. He gave direction to the conversation without being demanding.

JACK: It's important to get your reservations and doubts about the ways the project teams are working out on the table. Each of you should be able to say what is on your mind. Everyone should also feel free not to respond if it becomes difficult or uncomfortable. Openness is valued but so is the right of privacy.

After a slow beginning, something happened. Jim voiced concern about the progress in the meeting when Rod was present. "What's happened to us, Rod? Lately, we can't seem to get anywhere together on design problems." Rod replied, "Strange, I've noticed it too."

Rod went on to say that once Jim was promoted and no longer subordinate to him, Jim's whole philosophy of management seemed to change. Rather than promoting a free-wheeling atmosphere in the project team and building on novel ideas, no matter how far out, Rod saw Jim taking an "upper management" point of view. "I hear you say, 'Go slow, Rod. We don't want the boss upstairs to think we're on Cloud 9 and not anchored to reality.'"

Rod tried to clarify the misunderstanding, saying, "I'm really worried that we'll get a reputation for being hypothetical and impractical."

Other participants stepped in from time to time to assist the conversation. Jack supported the team by helping them over stalemates, clarifying, inviting views, and encouraged the emerging candor.

JIM: If you had let me know how you were reacting, we could have straightened this out long ago.

ROD: Well, I got the message you didn't care what I thought.

JACK: How do you see yourself as the leader of the project team? (speaking to Jim).

JIM: Well, I know it's our responsibility to come up with new projects, but part of the innovation is to evaluate what's going to be bought upstairs.

ROD: But Jim, you hardly let us develop an idea. Since you took over, I am nipped in the bud and others are, too. We don't get to toss something around, get others interested, take their thoughts into account, and come up with something that can see the light of day.

JACK: Do all the rest of you see it the way Rod does? (taking an informal test of opinion around the group).

(Nods of agreement came from everyone.) Well, Jim, I know you're concerned about higher level approval but you might consider a two-step approach in the next few meetings. Set aside time for an "anything goes" discussion. Thereafter, take a more hard-boiled look. How does that appear, Rod?

ROD: I'm not resisting evaluation. It's just that we need some breathing room.

JACK: Jim?

JIM: That will relieve my concern about going too far off track if everyone knows we're going to get to brass tacks later. I'll give it a try.

Each session seemed to bring about the same sort of suggestions for how their meetings might proceed. The consultant's presence was there, but his contributions were so unobtrusive that the team members had little awareness of their effect. As their confidence grew the team decided to terminate the consultant's service and "go it alone."

The first solo meeting went smoothly enough. Only one agenda item proved thorny and was laid over. The second solo meeting shifted agenda to deal with upcoming budget appropriations. It ended in an absolute stalemate.

As George closed the meeting, he felt a bitter dissatisfaction about the outcome. "When it comes to a crunch," he thought, "we can't really handle it yet. Maybe I should give Jack Clark a call. I'm sure he knows how to get us underway again."

Rationale

Catalytic interventions suffer the same sort of limitations as acceptant interventions. While the direction is subtly provided by the consultant, dependency continues because participative skills are not strengthened. In the vignette, the team finds value in removing procedural blockages, but discovers its weakness in participation when the consultant is not there.

Again, the issue of content is weak and the engineering of an outcome can appear as contrived. If the team senses an alliance between the leader and the consultant to direct a predetermined outcome, trust levels are likely to fall and the effectiveness of the process and the consultant will suffer.

It is hard to fire a gun slowly.

The Confrontational Approach

A confrontational approach is used when the consultant sees it as his or her job:

1. To point out which value assumptions are causing tensions or frictions
2. To challenge those who experience them to face one another and bring them to an end

The consultant may actually make the issue more intense so that team members cannot miss it. This is different than either reflecting or expressing feelings, the acceptant approach, or gathering of survey data, the facilitator approach. The confrontational approach forces people to identify the "real" values they need to "own up to" and say what needs to be said so that others can benefit from it. The member who is being challenged may be reluctant to be open about what is on his or her mind, but the goal is to get these values into the open where they can be reinforced or changed if needed.

The following is an example of a confrontative approach.

John Byron, management consultant, pushed open the heavy walnut door and entered the cool quiet of the president's office. Sam Miller turned away from his microcomputer screen, recognized his visitor, and stood up.

SAM: Glad to see you. I sure appreciate your coming down here on such short notice.

As you know, I want to initiate an executive initiatives program throughout the company. We have an annual meeting next month when we bring in our top 40 executives. I'd like you to address that meeting and help me to sell the program. I think it's essential to the future of this company. And it would bring meaning and substance to our future performance reviews. I've just now been reviewing last year's evaluations on the monitor and they're all pap—nice adjectives and all the scales rated about 0.7. With strategic initiatives, I could really get a handle on it and start to weed out the lightweights.

JOHN: (Shifting uneasily) Sam, I can't take that assignment, at least not with this format.

Sam stared incredulously. His neat plan to make a leap of progress now seemed at risk. He sensed that he couldn't pull it off alone; he needed the consultant's status and role as an independent authority. That was the only way to sell it; without that support, it was just another order — and a big one.

JOHN: Success of an executive initiative program results from personal commitment, not from knuckled-under compliance. You can't get that sort of commitment in one day.

Sam, I want to level with you. Your whole value system is one of authority–obedience. This executive initiative program is just another way to get control.

Sam had not expected this confrontation. He was completely off stride for a few moments as the words settled in. "John, you're saying you won't take a lucrative high-level assignment and help an old friend in the process?"

JOHN: Sam, I don't want to disappoint you, but I also don't think it would be a useful move to lead an old friend into a disaster. Even if I were effective in selling such a program to your management, little internal commitment would be generated. The initial enthusiasm would soon fade and behavioral change would not be substantive. Therefore, although I appreciate your invitation, I had better decline. It's in your interest too.

SAM: (Still unconvinced) John, you know this meeting is important. You are a "world-class" authority. Surely there is something useful you can do in a day.

JOHN: Okay. I can try, but not to sell the executive initiative program. I think the whole group needs to be aware of the pitfalls. Go ahead and convene your group, but let me raise these issues early on.

Four weeks later, the top executives meeting had just begun. It was the first session after the "early bird breakfast."

After a short introduction, John Byron, the consultant, addressed the group.

JOHN: I am not here to sell the merits of the executive initiative program but rather to discuss with you why I think it has a good likelihood of failing. (A stunned silence greeted his words.)

We need to approach this from the basis of the value systems in place in this company. Unless the operating values here in our top management group, at least as a point of departure, are congruent with those of the initiative value system, the strain of contradiction will cause the effort to crumble. The leadership and supervision in this company seem based on authority and obedience. Until we can confront that issue, you won't ever have an effective program to promote individual initiative.

The ensuing discussion was open and thoughtful. Together they began to design a program of action. John suggested that a positive basis for participation among the executive group would be to help them diagnose the problems they saw in the initiative program and to help them identify factors that might help or hinder its implementation. He felt that if he confronted them with the possibility that current leadership styles were not congruent with the program objectives they might take the first steps needed to effect development.

As the conversation continued, the group's awareness of

the issues began to displace the irritation they had felt when the consultant had confronted them.

Rationale

Confrontation involves facing up to a difference of opinion. That difference can include values, motives, facts, or perceptions. In the vignette, the consultant has challenged the client's value orientation by pointing to discrepancies between the value systems espoused in the initiative program and the authority–obedience values inherent in his client's leadership. The discussion that followed resulted in a positive basis for participation by the top executives rather than an imposed "hard sell" by the leader.

Even that course has risks, however. It may be seen as a clever introduction that salutes participation rather than as a real confrontation with the possibility that current leadership styles are incongruent with the value system inherent in a program that invites initiative.

Here, the first steps of realization have been taken. If the course can be maintained, a favorable outcome seems likely. Unfortunately reinforcement of participation skills is not apparent, and the organization may come to depend on the consultant to effect further confrontation and maintain the change process.

The Prescriptive Approach

The prescriptive approach is one in which the consultant comes in on an individual-by-individual basis. The consultant then studies:

1. The structure and assignments
2. The competencies of each individual team member

The agenda topics which are dealt with as a top team activity are also reviewed. Based on this, the consultant then prescribes how the organization could become stronger by doing things differently. Sample suggestions might be the addition of a new position, changes in organization reporting or responsibility, adjoining offices for all team members, or that meetings be held on Monday mornings rather than on Friday afternoon or less or more frequently. The consultant's recommendations may be more personal. For example, depending on the consultant's evaluation, the team leader may be told that he or she should be more directive or less directive.

The following is an example of a prescriptive approach.

The study had taken six months and the cost was $125,000.00. Now it lay in handsome multiring binders, one copy in front of each of the chairs on the conference table.

The president, Ken Thompson, entered the room with the two consultants in tow. Ken opened the meeting and introduced the consultants. As he turned the meeting over to them, one took his place at the overhead projector, the other at the screen. The one at the screen began.

"Well, gentlemen, I don't think I could add to what Ken has said. I think we should get right into the content of the report. Could I have the first slide, please!"

Two hours later, the presentation ended with the words, "and I want to thank you for all the support and assistance given so freely by your staff. Without it we could not have achieved the target deadlines. Are there any questions?" There were a few questions, none of substance.

Ken closed the meeting with the words, "I'm sure you'll

want a few days to review the report with your people. As you know, we plan to meet again two weeks from today. Thank you, gentlemen."

Three months later Ken met with Henry Thiboldt, vice president of human relations.

KEN: Henry, I want to talk to you about our reorganization report. As you know, we've spent a lot of money and to date there's been almost no progress in implementation. I'm afraid the data are cooling off. I really don't want to have to redo it but I'm getting a lot of excuses about changes in the market and in our principal competitor's strategy. Frankly, I'm worried.

HENRY: I don't know, Ken. I think it will be very difficult to put the changes into effect.

KEN: Well, difficult or not, I damn well mean to do it. What's the barrier and how do we overcome it?

HENRY: Participation, Ken. We haven't provided for it. By taking the report out of the hands of our managers and putting it into the hands of others, we violated what they consider to be their territory.

KEN: And now they are dragging their feet. I won't stand for it. They couldn't do it, so I had it done. Now I mean to have it implemented. I'm going to put it on the line at our meeting this week. I'll put their jobs on the line, too, if that's what it takes.

HENRY: Ken, you can do that but would it be wise? These are good people. They're not consciously rebelling. They weren't involved in the report and now they resist it—not consciously—they just don't feel any ownership. The result is they are afraid of moving on someone else's game plan.

After all, we are talking about restructuring the company.

KEN: Well, I plan to implement it. What do I need to do?

HENRY: Well, I think we could work up a program to get participation. I spoke to a consultant last week. You see, I rather imagined you would ask.

KEN: Another consultant? More cost? More time? Another prescription when we can't carry out the one we've got?

Rationale

Prescriptive interventions take the form of telling teams or members what to do. The value system of control and authority implicit in the use of external prescription is contradictory with seeking change through active participation.

At the point of impact between the change message and the existing team culture, several dynamics come into play:

1. People tend to resist imposed change.
2. Members feel that legitimately assigned territorial responsibility is invaded.
3. Coordination is prescribed by external agents.
4. Team members recognize the weaknesses in the existing status quo and quickly find explanations for why the new prescriptions "can't work".
5. Team members fail to factor into the prescription how the recommended changes might improve the existing status quo, thus they retain their resistance to the changes.

For these several reasons, the energy for implementation is often lacking. Knuckled-under compliance can be enforced—

and it frequently becomes the course for implementation. In the vignette, there is an emergent realization of the need for involvement. The course seems hopeful enough, but participation skills have not been addressed. Accordingly, the handling of inevitable conflicts during implementation will be from the same values and skills base that brought the team to the point of needing outside services in the first place.

The great advantages of the prescriptive solution are that expertise can be bought on an as-needed basis without a commitment for permanent employment. Because the prescription comes from "outside," it can be regarded as reflecting the best needs of the company rather than dressed-up vested interests. Furthermore, if the resources to implement the prescription are unavailable, they, too, can be brought in as needed.

The Parallel Organization or Collateral System

Still another approach that seeks to strengthen teamwork is called parallel organization or the collateral system. In this context parallel organization means a nonhierarchical grouping of people taking a fresh look at a problem without the constraints of territoriality, vested interests, or general discomfiture.

Let's use the parallel organization idea to help Ken implement his reorganization plan. We rejoin Ken and Henry at the point we left them.

HENRY: I don't think another consultant or another prescription will help here, Ken. It would just get us in all the deeper.

The issue of embracing the report is as important as the content of the report itself. It's not the quality of the report that's at stake. The major recommendation was to restructure the top teams of each function, moving the key players out of headquarters into the operating divisions. The members of the top teams themselves are dead set against it. It's a case of "team unbuilding" that is the source of resistance. There's a necessary price to pay to devise a delivery system to put the plan into place. We can drive it into place, but without support it will soon falter—and maybe we will too. I have a plan to reduce the resistance to change and maybe to get around it all together.

KEN: And?

HENRY: Well, we have to find a way to gain involvement in the change. And I think we must be alert to possibilities that that consultant's report can be improved on.

I suggest we appoint an in-house steering committee representing all managerial ranks. By reviewing the report for blind spots and inconsistencies with our needs, we can identify any major questions that need to be answered before we proceed. Smaller task forces can deal with those issues. Based on task force answers, the steering committee can attempt to formulate a sort of transcendent report that transforms the wisdom of the consultants into our own.

We may need some attention to vested interests but I think we can introduce cross-disciplinary committees to defuse intergroup rivalries, emotionality, and hidden goals. I think a parallel organization along those lines will put us in a position to implement.

KEN: If we do this, won't it result in some of the diehards gutting the report?

HENRY: No. The solution for that is to place at least one supportive person on each task force—and keep the diehards off. I promise you two things: the plan will be more to our liking and it will be implemented quickly.

KEN: Henry, I'm ready to give this plan of yours a shot. Can you be ready to present your parallel organization implementation ideas next week? I'd like to call a special meeting. And . . . (he pushed his copy of the consultant's reorganization report across the desk) take this. It sounds like you might need some extra copies.

Rationale

Parallel organizations take many different forms: task forces, matrix organizations, nonhierarchical functional teams, cross-disciplinary committees, and so on. These examples are used to depict the potentials in parallel organizations. This is basically a power strategy, and it invites the kinds of manipulations that Ken and Henry discussed—supporters on the task forces but no diehards. These kinds of hidden motivations can arouse organizationwide suspicion which is also a cause of resistance to change.

The basic notion underlying parallel organization is that an "uncommon" grouping of people allows an unencumbered view of the old culture. This permits a better look at the issues, disconnected from the standpoint of tradition, precedent, past practice, vested interest, and resistance to change. The new focus is on:

1. The character of the problem itself
2. What it will take to mobilize knowledgeable members of the organization

When such a prescriptive report is reexamined in this way, the traditional organization can be more effectively challenged by parallel organization members. The latter can demonstrate exactly how the recommendations in the prescriptive report might be implemented and the benefits to be derived from doing so.

On some occasions an additional aspect is required to overcome the team's resistance to the parallel organization's recommendations. This involves setting aside a period of time in which the teams from the traditional organization are called on to demonstrate how they would implement the solutions proposed by the parallel organization. In thinking through what they would do if they had to act according to the recommendations of the parallel organization, members of the traditional organization have to confront actual possibilities on an "as if" basis. Doing so often leads to the conviction that better results could be obtained if the parallel organization's recommendations are followed.

Summary

All the alternatives described in this chapter have a character of imposition about them. Leadership has perceived a need for change but sought to accomplish it *on* rather than through those affected. Change may be imperative, but authoritative imposition is likely to create problems of support at the important stage of implementation. True leadership involves creation of a vision of the possibilities; it also involves eliciting followership.

Chapter Fourteen

The Importance of Excellent Teamwork—Reprise

S ocial, economic, and technical changes increasingly impact on management teams everywhere. The old, easygoing ways of doing business are out. Any team that ignores
the need to consider its effectiveness faces the dilemma of
having its norms cast in the past and its plans cast in the
future.

· A team that understands that the new generation expects
  work to be fun is better able to attract top talent.
· A team that appreciates the changes needed to meet new
  challenges such as global competition and deregulation
  gains the benefit of facing up, being prepared, and being
  able to contend with a new set of able competitors.
· A team that grasps the possibilities of technology, instant
  information, and communication can run at the head of the
  race.

One of the major untapped resources of any commercial,
industrial, union, or governmental organization lies in the
dynamics of how people work together—in a word, teamwork. Teamwork has a quality of momentum about it. It pro-
ceeds in a straight line, uniform motion unless some mechanism of change alters its course.

The strategies of change include the following:

1. *Revolution.* Changing the team members in an attempt
   to acquire new value systems. Often a new set of problems is substituted for the old ones.

2. *Evolution.* Slow, steady steps of progress aimed at acquiring new skills and techniques. Often new fads that
   skirt the issues and leave underlying problems unre-
   solved are adopted.

2. *Theory-Based, Systematic Change.* Realization of a need, setting a model or ideal in place, and adopting one of several change methodologies to achieve it. This allows the most meaningful and permanent change.

The criteria of effective team building are straightforward:

1. The real issues need to be addressed.
2. Skills of effective participation are essential to ensure success.
3. Ongoing dependency on an outside source must not be created. Change that responds to the presence or absence of an outside party is elastic (i.e., it returns to its original state when the outside force is withdrawn).
4. Tips and techniques and fads add to the ever-present risk of self-delusion.
5. The effort must be active and participative. Little commitment is aroused by passive programs done on and not with the people involved.
6. There must be a results orientation. Satisfaction is transient without productivity.
7. Content and process must be integrated. Without content, process becomes self-serving and illusory; without process, content becomes fugitive and not self-sustaining.
8. A sense of outreach must prevail over introspective review of problems.

The steps to team effectiveness are simple:

1. Formulate a vision of the possibilities

2. Diagnose the present with self-delusion set aside

3. Close the gaps through an active process involving participative skills

We have come full circle. Spectacular teamwork has been illustrated and presented as a realistic possibility for any management team to aspire to—and for many teams to reach.

Appendix

Theory-Based Team Building

A n important beginning to theory-based team building is the creation of a shared model of what should be. An ideal model cast in operational terms provides a blueprint for the future to which all team members can subscribe.

Many change efforts falter because they are directed toward criticism of past actions rather than vision of the possibilities of the future. Criticism arouses resentment and fear and as a result is unlikely to arouse positive motivations of support and contribution.

Other change efforts fall short because there is no opportunity for team members to contribute in creating the vision. Vision is not the sole territory of the boss of the team. Even if he or she were the most imaginative and creative member of the team, there would be merit in exposing the vision to others to test for weakness and to allow the possibilities of strengthening.

Many leaders might pale at the thought of opening up the future direction to team review. Many would suspect the possibility of a self-serving direction which would become doubly hard to reverse. In fact, the risk is small.

An ideal culture instrument involving choice of each Teamwork Grid® style statement for 10 major aspects of organizational culture has been applied to several hundred thousand managers from cultural backgrounds as diverse as Japan, the United States, and Western Europe.

The 9,9 statement was selected as the ideal in over 85 percent of the individual responses. After group discussion the attraction to the 9,9 statement exceeded 99 percent. Experience suggests that the vision of the ideal is almost universally present and needs only to be aroused by the opportunity of contribution.

Designing the Model of What Should Be

An ideal model specifies what the conditions and results should be. To be ideal it must be uncontaminated by unjustified assumptions or extrapolations of the current condition.

Ideal thinking differs from idealistic thinking in that it can be tested against objective criteria to assess its practicality. Idealistic thinking has an unreal quality of subjective desires having little to do with the facts.

Ideal thinking is sometimes suspect and rejected as idealistic. Yet through history some of the world's greatest change projects — the Magna Carta and the U.S. Constitution — have come about because those who created them framed operational descriptions in ideal terms. The following 12 items identify properties of teamwork. The first step is for every member, including the boss, of the team to rank the seven alternatives from 7 for most ideal to 1, least ideal. The rankings are completed first by working individually. Then the entire team discusses and reaches agreement on the character of directions which is regarded as ideal for this team. The same is done for the other 11 items. When completed, the team has a blueprint of how it wishes to see teamwork carried out in terms of directions, meetings, job descriptions, delegation, and so on.

1. DIRECTIONS

IDEAL   ACTUAL

A _____   Directions come from the boss;   A _____
even though these may be re-
sisted, few efforts to change
them are successful.

IDEAL   ACTUAL

B _____   Suggestions keep work moving   B _____
            with the least friction among
            members; individual responsibil-
            ities are minimized and put in
            general terms that do not create
            pressure.

C _____   The boss determines the activi-   C _____
            ties to be accomplished and how
            they are to be done; members are
            treated well and compliance is
            expected in everyone's best inter-
            est.

D _____   Directions are minimal; action is D _____
            based mostly on doing things rit-
            ually or one thing at a time as
            new demands arise.

E _____   Adequate guidelines are pro-   E _____
            vided for accomplishing tasks;
            directions are tempered by con-
            sideration of individual resis-
            tances.

F _____   To be seen in the best possible   F _____
            light, directions from above are
            accepted without question but
            subordinates are provided de-
            tailed instructions to carry out
            orders with no deviations per-
            mitted.

G _____   Clear instructions for carrying out responsibilities are provided with opportunity available to clarify unclear areas; everyone understands what is to be done and why it is important.   G _____

2. MEETINGS

IDEAL   ACTUAL

A _____   Few meetings take place; when they do the exchanges are halfhearted with little give and take.   A _____

B _____   Usually an extension of previous topics, discussions convey the implicit assumption that majority thinking is to prevail.   B _____

C _____   Out of a desire to please and to avoid reprimand, members confine their participation to the boss-determined topics, rarely introducing other topics.   C _____

D _____   Discussion centers on personal concerns more than on team-centered issues.   D _____

IDEAL   ACTUAL

E _____   Action steps are reached by uti-   E _____
                lizing the resources of everyone
                who has something to contrib-
                ute.

F _____   A top-down approach predeter-   F _____
                mines meeting agenda. Team
                members offer information
                when requested; otherwise, ac-
                ceptance of topics is more or less
                passive or else actively resisted.

G _____   Members have hidden agenda   G _____
                designed to promote self-ad-
                vancement; one-to-one meetings
                are common even when issues
                discussed have teamwide signifi-
                cance.

3. CONFLICT

IDEAL   ACTUAL

A _____   Conflict is hidden or disguised as   A _____
                members maneuver to gain their
                objectives.

B _____   Members avoid taking positions   B _____
                that provoke conflict or becom-
                ing involved in those which exist.

C _____   When conflict arises members   C _____
                step in to soothe feelings and
                bring parties together.

IDEAL   ACTUAL

D _____   Points of disagreement are made   D _____
             explicit and reasons for them are
             identified to resolve underlying
             causes.

E _____   While members are thanked for   E _____
             expressing differing viewpoints,
             conflict is viewed as disruptive
             and terminated by the boss at the
             earliest opportunity.

F _____   Members sense when they have   F _____
             pushed their positions far
             enough and back off as neces-
             sary to meet others halfway.

G _____   Rank is used to cut off conflict   G _____
             and to decide between conflict-
             ing viewpoints; the disagreement
             goes underground.

4. OBJECTIVES

IDEAL   ACTUAL

A _____   More concern is placed on what   A _____
             members think and want than on
             achieving high performance ob-
             jectives for the team.

B _____   Objectives are couched in what-   B _____
             ever terms thought wanted by
             upper levels.

IDEAL		ACTUAL

C _____ Members are involved in setting, reviewing, and evaluating those objectives on which their performance can have an impact.   C _____

D _____ Objectives for results which are imposed are considered to be final.   D _____

E _____ Objectives are scaled to what members are prepared to accept.   E _____

F _____ Members are expected to accept enthusiastically the objectives assigned them.   F _____

G _____ Members work as they see fit with little examination of objectives or development of expectations for achieving them.   G _____

5. INNOVATION

IDEAL		ACTUAL

A _____ A positive attitude exists toward innovation, but new ideas are not really welcomed.   A _____

B _____ New ideas are accepted but then are unlikely to be acted on.   B _____

C _____ New ideas are not welcomed unless they can be used to elevate the status of the leader.   C _____

IDEAL		ACTUAL
D _____	Creativity and innovation are stimulated by the readiness to experiment.	D _____
E _____	Suggestions or novel ideas are resisted and the resistance is overcome only through persistent effort if at all.	E _____
F _____	New ideas which find acceptance are basically modifications of present ways of doing things.	F _____
G _____	Acceptance of ideas is intended to convey appreciation and support; whether or not they are relevant is secondary.	G _____

6. COMMUNICATION

IDEAL		ACTUAL
A _____	Members get the word on a "message-passing" basis; little in-depth discussion of job activities occurs.	A _____
B _____	Information is filtered or edited so that what is said is consistent with organization demands and other members' expectations.	B _____
C _____	Members are told what to do but in ways that encourage their acquiescence.	C _____

IDEAL   ACTUAL

D _____   Ideas and opinions are expressed   D _____
in a guarded fashion to avoid
seeming out of step and to avoid
exposure of weakness.

E _____   Social and nonwork topics make   E _____
the day pleasant; discussion of
work is incidental.

F _____   Members are well-informed and   F _____
participate in problem analysis
and decision making; differences are openly discussed and
worked through for sound understanding.

G _____   Communication is chiefly in the   G _____
form of directives on a need-to-
know basis; other than reporting, little information is sought
from members or others.

7. JOB DESCRIPTIONS

IDEAL   ACTUAL

A _____   Members are encouraged to in-   A _____
terpret their responsibilities in
ways that please them.

B _____   Members are unwilling to move   B _____
beyond narrow interpretations of
job description.

IDEAL   ACTUAL

C _____   Work assignments have evolved   C _____
               and are based more on tradition,
               precedent, and personality than
               on the nature of the tasks to be
               performed.

D _____   Responsibilities are designed   D _____
               around the nature of tasks and
               qualifications of members in
               ways that maximize interaction
               between those who share the ac-
               tion.

E _____   Responsibilities are outlined by E _____
               the boss to ensure control; team
               members frequently seek guid-
               ance even though it is not really
               needed.

F _____   Job responsibilities are compart- F _____
               mentalized; coordination among
               members is mostly through the
               formal chain of command.

G _____   Team members are defensive of   G _____
               their positions and seek to ex-
               pand their spheres of influence.

8. DELEGATION

IDEAL   ACTUAL

A _____   Degree of autonomy in complet-   A _____
               ing assignments is matched to

IDEAL   ACTUAL

individual capacity for exercising responsible interdependence.

B _____   Assignment of projects is me-   B _____
chanical with each member given
a "fair share" of the task within
limits of ability, time, or commitment.

C _____   Team members vie with one an-   C _____
other for choice assignments and
"plums."

D _____   The autonomy granted members   D _____
is reduced when they fail to meet
expectations.

E _____   Assignments are not planned;   E _____
they are handed out to whom-
ever is available.

F _____   Projects are implemented on the   F _____
basis of what each member pre-
fers to do rather than competence, time available, or priority
relative to other tasks.

G _____   Members have minimum lati-   G _____
tude in carrying out their assign-
ments; they are told what to
do—not why.

9. QUALITY

IDEAL | | ACTUAL

A _____ Quality standards are primarily a reflection of what the boss expects, and team members usually comply as directed. A _____

B _____ High quality standards receive full commitment from team members; outstanding performance is achieved and maintained because members are motivated to excel. B _____

C _____ Highest quality standards are emphasized; methods used to get them are not as important. C _____

D _____ Attitudes toward quality are that existing standards, even though allowing for deviations, are sufficient. D _____

E _____ Quality is saluted as a means of gaining recognition; actions do not reflect genuine concern for quality. E _____

F _____ Quality standards scarcely exist because they have never been established and/or refined. F _____

G _____ Standards of quality receive lip service but do not affect members' decisions or actions; gaining and maintaining approval of other members is more important.

10. PERFORMANCE APPRAISALS

IDEAL

ACTUAL

A _____ Performance reviews are centered on weaknesses and failures to measure up, emphasized at the expense of evaluating achievements.

A _____

B _____ Performance reviews are characterized by praise for compliance with directives and admonishments for shortcomings, but with the promise of restored good feelings when shortcomings have been corrected.

B _____

C _____ Performance appraisals are marked by compliments and positive affirmation with mistakes and errors rarely discussed.

C _____

D _____ Performance appraisals are perfunctory with little effort to dig into real issues of effectiveness.

D _____

E _____ Performance appraisals are based on previously jointly

E _____

Ideal   Actual

        agreed criteria with realistic re-
view of strengths and weak-
nesses on a two-way feedback
basis.

F _____   Performance reviews focus on   F _____
shortcomings which reflect ad-
versely on the team; to encourage greater effort, subordinates
are pitted against one another.

G _____   Criticisms are sandwiched in be-   G _____
tween praises and compliments.

11. TEAM SPIRIT

Ideal   Actual

A _____   There is a spirit of hail-fellow-   A _____
well-met, reinforced by "going
along to get along."

B _____   Members are more concerned   B _____
with self-preservation and protecting their own turf than with
teamwide activities.

C _____   This is a gathering of individuals   C _____
and not a team.

D _____   Interactions are warm and   D _____
friendly but this contributes little to strengthened performance.

IDEAL   ACTUAL

E _____   Favors are given with the implicit   E _____
             understanding they will be re-
             paid at an opportune time; sly
             ways of undercutting others to
             enhance one's own position are
             not uncommon.

F _____   Cohesion and team loyalty lead   F _____
             to mutual assistance when it is
             needed.

G _____   Coordination is ensured by the   G _____
             boss who encourages team mem-
             bers to accept what is asked of
             them in a loyal way and without
             complaints.

12. COMMITMENT

IDEAL   ACTUAL

A _____   Members are motivated to ad-   A _____
             vance their personal interests
             rather than to contribute to team
             or organizational goals.

B _____   When members discharge their   B _____
             duties and obligations as ex-
             pected of them, they are taken
             care of in a positive manner
             which contributes to their feel-
             ings of security.

IDEAL   ACTUAL

C _____   Commitment comes from mem-   C _____
                bers having a common stake in
                teamwide success; personal grat-
                ification is from making needed
                contributions.

D _____   Members are guided more by   D _____
                fear of being seen as disloyal or
                insubordinate than by team-cen-
                tered loyalty and commitment.

E _____   Commitment arises from the   E _____
                prestige of being a member in
                good standing of a "good orga-
                nization."

F _____   Commitment is from apprecia-   F _____
                tion of the human relations made
                possible through work.

G _____   Members stay because of pay   G _____
                and benefits; there is little loy-
                alty to organizational success.

Transfer your rankings for each item, pages _____, to the summary sheet below.

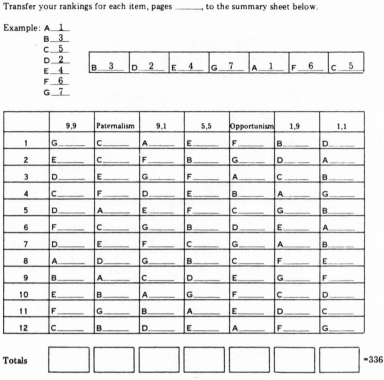

Example: A _1_
B _3_
C _5_
D _2_
E _4_
F _6_
G _7_

| B | 3 | D | 2 | E | 4 | G | 7 | A | 1 | F | 6 | C | 5 |

	9,9	Paternalism	9,1	5,5	Opportunism	1,9	1,1
1	G_____	C_____	A_____	E_____	F_____	B_____	D_____
2	E_____	C_____	F_____	B_____	G_____	D_____	A_____
3	D_____	E_____	G_____	F_____	A_____	C_____	B_____
4	C_____	F_____	D_____	E_____	B_____	A_____	G_____
5	D_____	A_____	E_____	F_____	C_____	G_____	B_____
6	F_____	C_____	G_____	B_____	D_____	E_____	A_____
7	D_____	E_____	F_____	C_____	G_____	A_____	B_____
8	A_____	D_____	G_____	B_____	C_____	F_____	E_____
9	B_____	A_____	C_____	D_____	E_____	G_____	F_____
10	E_____	B_____	A_____	G_____	F_____	C_____	D_____
11	F_____	G_____	B_____	A_____	E_____	D_____	C_____
12	C_____	B_____	D_____	E_____	A_____	F_____	G_____

Totals [ ] [ ] [ ] [ ] [ ] [ ] [ ] =336

Figure A.1. Ideal team culture summary.

Objective Appraisal of the "As Is" or Actual

The current actual status cannot be taken for granted. Team members may perceive it differently depending on their own values and the relationships and trust they experience. Situational management may particularly distort perceptions, since the boss may react differently to different team members. An objective scale is needed, together with a sharing of perceptions about what is really happening.

	9,9	Paternalism	9,1	5,5	Opportunism	1,9	1,1
1	G____	C____	A____	E____	F____	B____	D____
2	E____	C____	F____	B____	G____	D____	A____
3	D____	E____	G____	F____	A____	C____	B____
4	C____	F____	D____	E____	B____	A____	G____
5	D____	A____	E____	F____	C____	G____	B____
6	F____	C____	G____	B____	D____	E____	A____
7	D____	E____	F____	C____	G____	A____	B____
8	A____	D____	G____	B____	C____	F____	E____
9	B____	A____	C____	D____	E____	G____	F____
10	E____	B____	A____	G____	F____	C____	D____
11	F____	G____	B____	A____	E____	D____	C____
12	C____	B____	D____	E____	A____	F____	G____

Totals ☐ ☐ ☐ ☐ ☐ ☐ ☐ =336

Figure A.2. Actual team culture summary.

Using the same 12 items, each team member ranks the alternatives from 7, "most characteristic," to 1, "least characteristic." The boss and each member do this individually as prework. Team members then discuss their appraisal of the actual and reach explicit agreements among themselves as to what has been going on in the team on a day-by-day basis. Specific examples are needed to illustrate the actual situation in concrete terms, and then agree on the team ranking for "actual."

When the ideal is used as a spotlight to see the actual, objectivity about "what is" can be more readily attained. Without an ideal model for comparison, the actual properties of the situation are obscured by rationalization, self-deception, and ingrained habits. To change a situation those responsible for it must learn to describe it.

Discrepancies Between Actual and Ideal

By completing these two steps and comparing the ideal description, the actual discrepancies become evident between what exists and what is wanted. These discrepancies between actual and ideal are motivating. When discrepancies are identified, steps of development can then be planned and programmed for implementation in order to shift the character of teamwork from what has been to what team members have agreed they want to accomplish.

A deeper significance than appears on the surface comes sharply into focus when development is built on producing and closing gaps as a method of motivating change. There are two concepts of motivation here: tension reduction and financial and status rewards. Much organizational thinking is based on acceptance of the idea that financial and status rewards are the important motivators. But these alone appear insufficient to produce the tensions that motivate people to

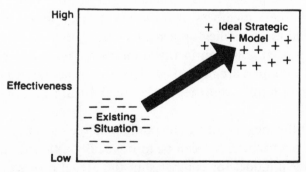

Figure A.3. Forces compelling action toward excellence.

search for solutions to problems. They may in fact even do precisely the opposite.

Many organizations give salary increases and promotions to those who best fit into an outmoded status quo. Then the reward system is unlikely to motivate actions to change. But there are psychological factors in all problem situations that appear to be important for stimulating creativity and innovative problem solving. When a clear-cut discrepancy between what is and what should be is recognized, shared tensions arise that focus thoughts, efforts, and feelings on how to resolve the matter to eliminate the contradiction.

Such tensions provide a motivational force that compels members to solve those problems that pose barriers to team performance. Through understanding the force of these tensions, teams can make deliberate use of them, harnessing energy in the direction of synergistic results and spectacular teamwork.

The ideal model is complete only when it takes into consideration all identifiable forces bearing on the team of the corporation. These include not only the forces that are directly controlled by team members themselves but also the outside environment within which the team is embedded and under the influence of which it must operate. What this means is that there are likely to be constraints over which the team has little or no control such as fixed budget or other teams from whom cooperation is needed to be fully productive. The model also needs to take these outside-of-the-team-itself factors into consideration for their actual impact for whether steps might be taken to create a more favorable environment for the team.

Steering, Correction, and Critique Mechanisms

Merely setting change steps in motion does not necessarily ensure that the actions needed for converting from the actual to the ideal will be successfully implemented. Steering, correction, and critique mechanisms are indispensable for guiding development. If teamwork is measured before development is initiated and at various points after team building takes place, then information is available to steer action as well as to determine results. Team members can identify factors in the situation impeding progress and unsuspected weaknesses or limitations in their model of teamwork. Sign of drag and drift can be anticipated and corrected.

This approach to team building has several advantages. One is that it relies on theory as the basis for developing a sound model of teamwork. It arouses enthusiasm for change rather than resistance to it. One limitation on the magnitude of change that is possible through theory-based team development is in the capacity of people to reason about their problems. Risk of failure is reduced because the proposed changes enjoy shared agreement and can be evaluated for their probable consequences before implementation is started. Another limitation is that many managers prefer the excitement of fire fighting to the conceptual activity and commitment that systematic development calls for.

Summary

What have teams achieved when they have completed team building? First, they have a model of excellence of teamwork against which to judge their present effectiveness. A model of excellence in teamwork opens up gaps between what is and what should be. It creates conditions under which goals and objectives can be set for closing these gaps. Next, each member has a clear standard for setting objectives to increase his or her personal effectiveness. Team members have a deepened sense of the importance of candor for getting their operational problems on the table and resolving them. They have a greater readiness to face the conflicts that result when problems that need to be solved are tackled. When people become aware of the extent to which their own history, traditions, precedents, and past practices, as embedded in their patterns and habits of work, have reduced their effectiveness, they begin to realize what must be done to get performance on a problem-solving basis.

Index

Index